STUDY GUIDE
BEVERLEY BLOIS

NINTH EDITION

A HISTORY OF CIVILIZATION

VOLUME I: PREHISTORY TO 1715

ROBIN W. WINKS

CRANE BRINTON
JOHN B. CHRISTOPHER
ROBERT LEE WOLFF

Prentice Hall, Upper Saddle River, New Jersey 07458

© 1996 by PRENTICE-HALL, INC.
Simon & Schuster / A Viacom Company
Upper Saddle River, New Jersey 07458

All rights reserved

10 9 8 7 6 5 4 3 2 1

ISBN 0-13-228404-9
Printed in the United States of America

Contents

Preface v

1. The First Civilizations 1
2. The Greeks 9
3. The Romans 17
4. Judaism and Christianity 24
5. The Early Middle Ages in Western Europe 29
6. Byzantium and Islam 36
7. Church and Society in the Medieval West 42
8. The Beginnings of the Secular State 48
9. The Late Middle Ages in Eastern Europe 56
10. The Rise of the Nation 62
11. The Renaissance 68
12. The Protestant Reformation 75
13. The Great Powers in Conflict 81
14. Exploration and Expansion 87
15. The Problem of Divine-Right Monarchy 92

Preface

The introductory history survey remains an important element in the general education curriculum of most colleges and universities. The fortunes of "survey courses" have ebbed and flowed but, since their introduction in the 1920s and 1930s, courses in the history of civilization in American institutions of higher education have proved durable. Since our nation's entry into world affairs approximately seventy-five years ago, it has become far more important than earlier for Americans to frame a credible and usable story of Europe, past and present. Especially for university students, few courses have as much potential for breaching what Bertrand Russell called "the tyranny of the local" as the civilization survey.

Textbooks abound which condense the human past "from Plato to NATO" or, even more heroically, from the Pleistocene to the modern scene. None, however, is more highly regarded or widely used than the one which this guide is designed to accompany. The Winks, Brinton, Christopher, Wolff text in the history of civilization remains, over thirty years after the introduction of its first edition, one of the most powerful and "friendly" mediators between American students and the study of the human past. Professor Robin Winks' revisions and updating for the current, ninth edition enhance the elegance and breadth of coverage which remain the strength of the text's narrative.

The primary function of this guide is to provide students and their instructors with exercises designed to review important factual and interpretative statements and passages in the text. For this reason, the text is frequently quoted or paraphrased in the exercises, many of which are designed to call students' attention, a second time, to particular descriptions of or propositions about people and events. It is hoped that by this reiteration of brief but important passages, the guide may be helpful for reviewing the text material, whether or not the self-check exercises are systematically completed. Besides the exercises and key terms, there are two additional elements in the guide: a chapter overview, introducing every chapter, which attempts to synthesize its contents; and brief discussions, in some but not all chapters, of the illustrations, documents, maps, and photographs which the text authors have carefully chosen to complement their history.

Beverly Blois
Northern Virginia Community College, Loudoun Campus

CHAPTER 1

The First Civilizations

Overview: Anthropologists and archaeologists tell us that, since the appearance of our human ancestors, the species has lived three very different lifestyles: nomadic hunters, settled farmers, and city dwellers. Town life, or civilization, and the writing of history have traveled together through the last five thousand years, forming a record of human hopes, fears, and accomplishments on which this guide, and the textbook it accompanies, is based.

Before history, there was a time, until about 10,000 years ago, when nomadism was state-of-the-art for everybody. Because of the low population density this regime demands, the earth was thinly but evenly peopled during the Old Stone Age. Then, while some continued to live as nomads, others began to settle in communities and work the soil, giving birth to agriculture and to the era of the New Stone Age. By 3000 B.C., some of these communities had become large and complex enough to merit the term "town" or "city." At about the same time, writing evolved as a necessary skill for some people living the increasingly complex urban lifestyle, and with the conscious, written chronicling of human accomplishment, ends the long period known as prehistory.

Histories of civilization, this one included, normally begin their story with the Sumerians, a southern Mesopotamian people who loom large in the development and diffusion of social institutions and mentalities. This continuity is especially apparent in the other Mesopotamian societies, but the Sumerians seem also to have stimulated, by their example, developments in the Nile valley and elsewhere.

KEY TERMS FOR DISCUSSION

prehistory	slavery
Paleolithic Era	alphabet
Mesopotamia	monotheism
hydraulic society	prophecy
ziggurat	Iliad

SELF-CHECK EXERCISES: After reading the chapter, you may wish to monitor your retention of the material with the following questions.

1. According to the text, which most distinguishes history from prehistory?

    a. settled communities
    b. writing
    c. long-distance trade
    d. religion

2. The east African area where a series of archaeological discoveries in the 1950s-1960s revolutionized views of early man was

    a. the Kenya highlands
    b. Mt. Kilimanjaro
    c. the Congo basin
    d. the Olduvai gorge

3. True Homo sapiens appeared approximately when?

    a. 2,000,000 years ago
    b. 500,000 years ago
    c. 37,000 years ago
    d. 12,000 years ago

4. Which one factor most distinguishes the Neolithic from the Paleolithic era?

    a. the calendar
    b. farming
    c. metallurgy
    d. cave painting

5. Which was not a feature of Hammurabi's code of law?

   a. capitalism
   b. social stratification
   c. polygamy
   d. leniency

6. Which was not a characteristic of ancient Egypt?

   a. a deep historical sense
   b. a hydraulic society
   c. dynamism and optimism
   d. rulers regarded as gods

7. An early investigator of Knossos and the Linear B script was

   a. A. Evans   c. F. Petrie
   b. H. Schliemann   d. P. Botta

8. Which, according to the text, marks the end of the Greek Dark Age?

   a. iron replacing bronze
   b. virtual disappearance of literacy
   c. composition of the Iliad and Odyssey
   d. Greek migrations to Asia Minor

For questions 9. through 20., select, from the choices provided, the individual or society described or the source quoted.

9. Here, in the Jordan Valley, during the 1950s, archaeologists excavated a town radiocarbon-dated at about 7800 B.C. that had extended over about eight acres and included perhaps three thousand inhabitants.

   a. Jericho   c. Jarmo
   b. Tepe Yahya   d. Catal Huyuk

10. Well established by the year 3000 B.C., they had invented bronze and made tools and weapons of it. They had begun to accumulate and use capital and, perhaps most important, they adapted writing into a flexible tool of communication.

    a. Philistines   c. Sumerians

     b. Akkadians   d. Elamites

11. Their ruler reached both the Black Sea and the Mediterranean on a conquering expedition north and west, after which he boasted that he had become "lord of the world." Their militarism was harsh, and they regularly transported into captivity the entire population of defeated cities.

    a. Chaldeans   c. Assyrians
    b. Sumerians   d. Medes

12. These five centuries saw extraordinary advances. In foreign affairs, the Egyptians engaged in a struggle for Syria and Palestine, and established their own network of local governors in their conquered territories. They embarked on a vast building program that depended on a ready supply of forced labor.

    a. old Kingdom   c. Middle Kingdom
    b. Hyksos era   d. New Kingdom

13. He caused a major internal upheaval by challenging the priests of the sun god Amen in an effort to impose monotheism on Egypt. He ruled from a new capital in Amarna, which gives its name to the "Amarna heretics" who believed in "one true god."

    a. Ramses II   c. Thutmose I
    b. Akhenaten   d. Tutankhamen

14. "When the seventh day dawned the storm from the south subsided, the sea grew calm, the flood was stilled: I looked at the face of the world and there was silence, all mankind was turned to clay."

    a. Gilgamesh   c. Amarna letters
    b. Genesis   d. Book of the Dead

15. Women were not fully subordinated to men: they could own property and, under certain conditions, inherit it; they might also enter into business agreements. Most unusual in ancient societies, women could succeed to the throne.

    a. Egypt   c. Sumer
    b. Babylon   d. Persia

16. After 1300 B.C., they flourished along the south coast of what is now Lebanon, carrying on a brisk trade with the western Mediterranean, founding Citium and Carthage as colonies. They brought their Semitic tongue (Punic) more than halfway to the Straits of Gibraltar, through which their ships had often sailed.

  a. Philistines   c. Canaanites
  b. Phoenicians   d. Hittites

17. As outsiders battering their way into Canaan against the entrenched resistance of those already there, the confederation of tribes was held together by their new religion. Gradually, by ruthless conquest, they added to their holdings, and their confederation became a monarchy around 1020 B.C.

  a. Assyria   c. Phoenicia
  b. Philistia   d. Israel

18. A busy maritime people whose ships not only plied the Mediterranean but presumably managed to defend the island against invaders (since none of their palaces was fortified), they had garrisons and even colonies abroad--a Bronze Age overseas empire on a small scale exacting tribute from others.

  a. Mycenaeans   c. Minoans
  b. Dorians   d. Hurrians

19. A largely barren land, mountainous and divided into small valleys and plains separated from each other, with none far from the sea, its inhabitants took advantage of the rugged coasts and islands to sail from place to place, profiting by the exchange of olive oil and wine for grain and metal and slaves.

  a. Crete   c. Greece
  b. Anatolia   d. Palestine

20. Despite a few experiments elsewhere, they were the first to insist that theirs was the only and universal god.

  a. Babylonians   c. Jews
  b. Egyptians   d. Assyrians

USING THE CHAPTER'S DOCUMENTARY AND VISUAL RESOURCES

On page 12, see the boxed document: The Code of Hammurabi is one of many ancient Near Eastern codes of law. It was based on Mesopotamian examples from at least 300 years before its own composition around 1750 B.C., and would itself serve as a model for subsequent Biblical codes. Babylonian artists depicted Hammurabi receiving the code, already incised on a tablet of clay or stone, from the god Marduk, a scene which may have formed the basis of the story of Moses receiving the stone tablets of commandments.

The Code of Hammurabi may rightly be called "stern," as the text states. It is replete with examples of "an eye for an eye" justice, called lex talionis in legal terminology.

FOR DISCUSSION: While reading the laws themselves, make notes of provisions indicative of the following--discrimination against women, discrimination against the lower classes, lex talionis, capital punishment, roles for women other than wife and mother, business and contracts.

On pages 15 and 16, see the images of Akhenaten and Nefertiti: The first married couple in history about whom more than a few words may accurately be written, Akhenaten and Nefertiti stand out in both visual and literary sources from the years around 1350 B.C., when, in a series of actions that are often termed revolutionary, Akhenaten, apparently with the assistance of his "great royal wife," shifted the focus of Egyptian art, religion, and politics. The image of Akhenaten is one of the most characteristic poses of Egyptian monarchs--wearing the headdress intended to resemble a lion's mane, clutching the crook and flail (symbols of what today might be termed "carrot and stick" leadership), and staring impassively into eternity. The almost caricatured depiction of his features is, however, decidedly untraditional in Egyptian art, unique to the Amarna art of Akhenaten's reign. Nefertiti, on the other hand, is treated realistically, a tendency in most Egyptian art, and one that obviously also flourished at the time.

While much is known about the royal couple, the problematics of their reign (many authorities feel Nefertiti was, for at least several years, co-ruler with her husband) far exceed the certainties. It is not known, for instance, whether Nefertiti was Egyptian or foreign-born, or why, several years before Akhenaten's death, all references to her disappear. The Egyptians' disinclination to write their own history is frequently maddening!

FOR DISCUSSION: Consider prospects for the long-run survival of Akhenaten's projects, a flurry of innovations in the face of conservative Egyptian traditionalism. Compare Egypt's Amarna period with other examples of rapid social, political, and/or cultural change.

ANSWER KEY, WITH PAGE REFERENCES IN THE TEXT

	Answer	Page
1.	b	5
2.	d	5
3.	c	5
4.	b	7
5.	d	12
6.	a	13
7.	a	22
8.	c	24
9.	a	7
10.	c	9
11.	c	12
12.	d	14
13.	b	14
14.	a	11
15.	a	16
16.	b	18
17.	d	19
18.	c	20
19.	c	21
20.	c	19

CHAPTER 2

The Greeks

Overview: With the Greeks, modern societies begin to see themselves mirrored in the life of a people of antiquity. Whole realms of endeavor, familiar to us, were not only equally familiar to the ancient Greeks, but were for them, no less than for us, subject to much commentary and reflection. Politics, from the Greek polis (city), and economics, from ecos (household), are just two examples. Also indicative of the Greek penchant for categorization and systematization of thought and activity are the many survivals of the Greek language in the modern academic (itself a Greek term) curriculum: poetry, music, biology, physics, history, and mathematics are some disciplines originating with the inquiries of the Greeks, who also saw athletics (yet another of their concepts) as an integral component of education.

The political history of the Greeks is preserved in sufficiently full and rich detail that it has formed a corpus of object lessons for all subsequent western peoples, beginning already with the Romans. The allure of certain places and moments in the Greek experience remains pronounced. When Voltaire adjudged classical Athens one of the four or five truly exciting, not to mention great, periods in the history of civilization, he was expressing a commonly held view.

In the time of Alexander the Great, the accomplishments of the "Golden Age" of Greece were consolidated into a portable body of knowledge and were spread throughout the eastern end of the Mediterranean and beyond into what are today India, Pakistan, and the Soviet Union. Rome, too, would soon form part of the Hellenistic cultural ecumene, and would pass its essence forward to medieval Europe.

KEY TERMS FOR DISCUSSION

polis	Hellenization
aristocracy	hubris
democracy	history
ostracism	rhetoric
Delian League	stoicism
hegemony	

SELF-CHECK EXERCISES: After reading the chapter, you may wish to monitor your retention of the material with the following questions.

1. Our understanding of Greek theology comes largely from

    a. Hesiod
    b. Homer
    c. Pericles
    d. Pindar

2. In Greek cities, the public gathering place (and market area) was the

    a. acropolis
    b. agora
    c. ecclesia
    d. ecos

3. Invention of coinage is attributed, in the text, to

    a. Corinth
    b. Byzantium
    c. Lydia
    d. Phoenicia

4. In the Spartan experiment with self-sufficiency, or autarky, most of the society's work was done by the

    a. homoioi
    b. perioikoi
    c. hoplites
    d. helots

For items 5. through 8., give the name of the person who is either described or who is the speaker in the following quotations and paraphrases from the text. Choose from the following individuals:

Draco   Isocrates

Cleisthenes   Pericles

Pisistratus   Solon

5. _____ He canceled current debts, published a new constitution, and tried to improve the general prosperity by emphasizing the need to abandon complete economic dependence on agriculture. He even offered citizenship to non-Athenians who would come to the city to work. By introducing quasi-democratic innovations while retaining aristocratic election of the rich... and the oligarchic power of the few ... he had introduced a radical set of compromises.

6. _____ Having come to power as the leader of the poor, he gave them loans, embarked on a lavish program of public works to be sure there were jobs for all, subsidized the arts, and increased the magnificence of state religious celebrations. His sons followed his policies, but... opposition continued and the government grew more tyrannical ....

7. _____ Using a new basic political unit, the <u>deme</u>, he ordered all citizens to be registered as voters within their demes, irrespective of their origins .... He also rezoned Attica into three new regions, inventing a fundamental tool of democracy--the gerrymander.

8. _____ "Our constitution does not copy the laws of neighboring states; we rather are a pattern to others than imitators ourselves. Its administration favors the many instead of the few: this is why it is called a democracy ....Instead of looking on discussion as a stumbling block in the way of action, we think it an indispensable preliminary .... In short I say we are the school of Hellas."

9. Generally powerless and confined, Athenian women did exercise considerable authority over

        a. religion   c. the household
        b. the agora   d. politics

10. While most Athenian officials were chosen by lot, which were elected?

    a. archons   c. council members
    b. generals   d. phratries

11. Battle at which 300 Spartans delayed, perhaps decisively, Xerxes' advance south into Greece:

    a. Marathon   c. Thermopylae
    b. Salami   d. Leuctra

12. Which was not among Pericles' actions as nominal leader of Athens?

    a. pay for officeholders
    b. limitations on citizenship
    c. construction of the Parthenon
    d. ended Athenian imperialism

13. During the Peloponnesian War, the Athenian leader most identified with compromise and peace was

    a. Nicias   c. Cleon
    b. Alcibiades   d. Thucydides

14. "His career vividly illustrates the vulnerability of the Athenian democracy to a plausible, charming, talented scoundrel." This is the assessment, in the text, of

    a. Pericles   c. Alcibiades
    b. Themistocles   d. Phidias

15. According to the text, the inability of 4th century Greek cities to give up internecine war owed principally to

    a. general prosperity
    b. the Pelopponesian League
    c. decline of slavery
    d. decline of Thebes

16. He applied Theban military principles to his army and led it in person; to get money he exploited gold and silver mines and minted his own coinage; in 338, he totally defeated the Athenian-Theban alliance, but by sparing Athens he disproved the fears of Demosthenes; he seemed a kind of Homeric hero in the flesh almost a thousand years after the siege of Troy. This is the text's description of

    a. Epaminondas
    b. Lysander
    c. Philip
    d. Alexander

17. Alexander campaigned in all but which of these areas

    a. Egypt
    b. Persia
    c. India
    d. Italy

18. According to the text, the most important aspect of Alexander's career was his

    a. ruthlessness
    b. megalomania
    c. attempt to form a single, hellenized world state
    d. identification with Achilles

19. The Greek goddess of fertility and harvests, whose name literally means "earth mother," was

    a. Demeter
    b. Diana
    c. Diogenes
    d. Dodona

20. The historian who recorded Pericles' "Funeral Oration" was

    a. Thucydides
    b. Herodotus
    c. Themistocles
    d. Xenophon

21. The tragedian whose most famous trilogy dealt with the family of Oedipus was

    a. Aristophanes
    b. Euripides
    c. Aeschylus
    d. Sophocles

22. "Women sexually denied themselves to their husbands until the men made peace" in the play <u>Lysistrata</u> by

    a. Menander   c. Pindar
    b. Aristophanes   d. Arrian

23. In the text, the phrase "father of history" is used to describe

    a. Herodotus   c. Xenophon
    b. Thucydides   d. Polybius

24. The first Greek thinker to use the term <u>cosmos</u> was

    a. Eratostheses   c. Hippocrates
    b. Pythagoras   d. Aristarchus

25. Plato's best-known student, who concerned himself with "matters as they are" and pioneered the scientific method was

    a. Socrates   c. Aristotle
    b. Epicurus   d. Diogenes

==

USING THE CHAPTER'S VISUAL RESOURCES

<u>On pages 40 and 61, see the maps of Alexander's and Rome's empires</u>: Alexander the Great, inspired by the literary example of Achilles, whom he also believed to be his ancestor, set out at age 22 to conquer parts of the Persian Empire. When he died at age 33, he had accumulated all of Achaemenid Persia and more, including substantial parts of today's India, Pakistan, and Soviet Central Asia, into one of history's largest and certainly its most quickly assembled empire.

    Greco-Macedonian hegemony gave way to Roman imperium, encompassing a slightly larger domain than Alexander's, but maintaining authority therein for hundreds of years (Alexander's empire had crumbled upon his death). If Alexander's idol was the mythical Achilles, Rome's was the historical Alexander, dead only fifty years when Rome's expansion beyond Italy was beginning. Alexander's legendary successes haunted the greatest and most ambitious, as well as the most despicable, of Rome's leaders: Caesar's assassination brought to an end his plans to retrace Alexander's route in the

East; Augustus, like Caesar, visited Alexander's tomb; Caligula was satisfied to wear the breastplate of Alexander, as was Nero to be compared with him by obsequious Greek politicians; Trajan sorrowfully compared his own advanced age and, comparatively minor, accomplishments with Alexander's youthful conquests. It was the Romans, always under the spell of Alexander's prior endeavors and constantly justifying themselves with reference to his example, who first termed him magnus, "the great." As subsequent empires have measured themselves against Rome, Rome measured itself against him.

The institutions which enabled the Pax Romana to withstand the test of five centuries and to pass forward to Medieval Europe a linguistic and religious infrastructure--Roman law, military policy, and public administration--are absent from the territories conquered by Alexander, who, if he intended to establish such institutions, died before doing so. The single greatest question about the life and times of Alexander, about whom so much is known, concerns his motives for the newly won empire. Was he, as the most heroic of his biographers assert, attempting to establish, by a fusion of Greek and Persian elements, a large, humanistic, multinational polity? The impossibility of answering the question definitively adds to the considerable intrigue of Alexander, whose early death has spawned speculation about what might have been for almost 2500 years.

FOR DISCUSSION: In light of your own knowledge of Alexander, do you consider him to have been on a "civilizing" mission, or to have been simply interested in conquest? Attempt to appraise other examples of imperialism by this standard. Looking at the maps, list some nations which were exposed to one or more, or to none, of the following empires: Macedonian, Persian, Roman. Frame some tentative conclusions concerning cultural, political, and linguistic legacies.

ANSWER KEY, WITH PAGE REFERENCES IN THE TEXT

	Answer	Page
1.	a	27
2.	b	28
3.	c	29
4.	d	29
5.	Solon	30
6.	Pisistratus	30
7.	Cleisthenes	30
8.	Pericles	34
9.	c	31
10.	b	33
11.	c	33
12.	d	34
13.	a	35
14.	c	36
15.	a	37
16.	c	38
17.	d	40
18.	c	39
19.	a	42
20.	a	35
21.	d	42
22.	b	43
23.	a	44
24.	b	45
25.	c	46

CHAPTER 3

The Romans

Overview: Many people automatically associate the words "decline and fall" with the society and civilization of the Romans, but we should remember that it is the magnitude of Rome's achievement that makes its demise such a turning point in history. Roman power, or imperium, spread to an unprecedented extent in time and space. For a thousand years, the Romans were either acquiring or maintaining control of the entire Mediterranean coastline, not to mention extensive territorial holdings in Europe, Africa, and Asia. Roman rule made the Mediterranean a secure and private lake. Mare Nostrum, our sea, the Romans called it, a maritime highway over which passed the extensive commerce that provided an economic justification for Roman power.

The Romans bequeathed three great legacies to subsequent times: language, law, and religion. Latin became parent to half a dozen modern European languages; Roman law has been drawn upon ceaselessly by politicians and jurists (including the writers of the U. S. constitution); and Roman religion, which very late in imperial history became Christianity, became the cultural center of gravity for Medieval Europe.

The Romans were great consolidators of political power, but this did not prevent them from also sharing political and citizenship rights with most of the empire's constituent nationalities, accomplishing history's first functional toleration of national differences and realizing a pragmatic "humanism" which may have been what Alexander intended for his own empire. With Rome, ancient civilization reached both its high point and terminus, though the subsequent medieval civilization, born in the "wild West" of the empire, would have been unimaginable without its deep Roman roots.

KEY TERMS FOR DISCUSSION

republic

imperium

toga candida

latifundia

romance languages

Pax Romana

tetrarchy

pontifex maximus

SELF-CHECK EXERCISES: After reading the chapter, you may wish to monitor your retention of the material with the following questions.

1. Fifth century B.C. republican Rome most resembled

    a. 4th century Macedonia
    b. 5th century Sparta
    c. 6th century Athens
    d. 3rd century Alexandria

2. Under the Roman republic, plebeians gained political power through all but which of the following:

    a. the right to their own officials, the tribunes
    b. the right to their own public gathering, the tribal assembly
    c. the abolition of debt slavery
    d. establishing their own city outside Rome

3. According to the text, which was characteristic of Roman, but not Greek, women?

    a. infant girls were sometimes abandoned
    b. practice of contraception and abortion was frequent
    c. most women avoided public life
    d. they are seldom mentioned in contemporary written accounts

4. Hannibal accomplished all but which of the following:

    a. brought his army over the Alps into Italy
    b. campaigned in Italy for fifteen years
    c. besieged Rome itself
    d. escaped after defeat at battle of Zama

5. Which was not characteristic of late republican Roman agriculture?

   a. spread of latifundia
   b. absence of slavery
   c. intensive farming
   d. large-scale cattle ranching

6. The reforms of the brothers Gracchi sought all but which of the following:

   a. resettlement of landless farmers
   b. construction of roads and granaries
   c. urban poor relief
   d. preservation of big landowners' powers

For items 7. through 11., give the name of the person who is described in the following quotations or paraphrases from the text.

Pompey	Augustus
Catiline	Caesar
Cicero	Tiberius
Marius	Caligula
Antony	Claudius

7. _____ The first of the Roman generals to achieve power, as leader of the populares, he had himself elected as consul five times in succession. He reorganized the army, abolishing the requirement that a Roman citizen must pay for his own equipment--a rule that had automatically excluded the poor.

8. _____ In 49 B.C., he defied an order from the Senate to give up his command and stay in Gaul, and he led his loyal troops south across the Rubicon River boundary, beginning a civil war .... He took the title "Liberator," and his dictatorship was twice renewed, on the second occasion for life.

9. _____ He had fallen in love with Cleopatra, who bore him three children. After a victory over the Parthians in 34 B.C., he made his bid for empire, but after the defeat at Actium in 31 B.C.,

he fled to Alexandria and committed suicide.

10. _____ He was consul, imperator, and princeps (his regime is called the principate). Since he called himself the restorer of the republic, Romans could still feel that they were again living under republican rule. He created a civil service open to men of talent, initiated the most careful censuses known to that time, and wished, as he said, to turn Rome from a city of brick to a city of marble.

11. _____ The best of the first four emperors to succeed Augustus, he was a learned student of history and languages who strove to imitate Augustus by restoring cooperation with the Senate. He improved the bureaucracy and generously granted citizenship to provincials. To Rome's territories, he added Britain.

12. Roman taste, and money, led to some of the most noted buildings of antiquity, when wedded to the architectural skills and styles of

    a. Greece   c. Persia
    b. Egypt   d. Macedonia

13. "The procurator of Judea, Pontius Pilate, allowed the execution by crucifixion of Jesus, who called himself 'the Anointed,'" in the reign of

    a. Nero   c. Augustus
    b. Tiberius   d. Caligula

14. According to the text, Roman Italy was one of only five significant slave-based societies in history, in company with all but which of the following:

    a. Mogul India   c. antebellum U.S. South
    b. Brazil   d. classical Athens

15. As a member of the First Triumvirate, Caesar achieved great military successes in

    a. Greece   c. Parthia
    b. Gaul   d. Sicily

16. He simultaneously held the titles imperator, consul, and princeps.

   a. Caesar
   b. Augustus
   c. Trajan
   d. Vespasian

17. The era of the five good emperors (A.D. 98-180) includes the reigns of all but

   a. Hadrian
   b. Antoninus
   c. Commodus
   d. Nerva

18. "The primary function of [Roman] women was determined by the state to be biological. Once having fulfilled that function, they were often free to play other and more independent roles....., in all but which of the following areas:

   a. business
   b. management of slaves
   c. schooling
   d. politics

19. "A cultivated Stoic philosopher who found no pleasure at all in his powers as emperor, his melancholy <u>Meditations</u> (written in Greek) serve as a corrective to official optimism." Who is being described?

   a. Trajan
   b. Valens
   c. Hadrian
   d. Marcus Aurelius

20. The reforms of Diocletian, fundamental to the "New Empire," included all but which of the following:

   a. made his headquarters in Asia Minor
   b. decreed toleration of Christianity
   c. adopted trappings of oriental monarchy
   d. attached agriculturists to the soil

21. According to Edward Gibbon, the principal cause of Rome's decline was

a. Christianity's erosion of civic spirit
   b. economic pressure of the underprivileged
   c. influx of Greeks and orientals
   d. dependence on slavery

22. The concepts "natural law" and "law of nations" are integral to the humanist philosophy of

   a. Lucretius   c. Cicero
   b. Vergil   d. Terence

23. His Germania extolled the virtues of a "barbarian" society and was "an acid commentary on the Romans' descent into the love of luxury for its own sake":

   a. Tacitus   c. Suetonius
   b. Livy   d. Ovid

24. During Augustus' tenure, Rome's European frontier became the river

   a. Rhone   c. Rhine
   b. Thames   d. Seine

25. His rule inaugurated the Pax Romana.

   a. Diocletian   c. Hadrian
   b. Marcus Aurelius d. Augustus

ANSWER KEY, WITH PAGE REFERENCES IN THE TEXT

	Answer	Page
1.	c	52
2.	d	53
3.	b	53
4.	c	54
5.	b	55
6.	d	56
7.	Marius	56
8.	Caesar	57
9.	Antony	58
10.	Augustus	59
11.	Claudius	60
12.	a	71
13.	b	60
14.	a	55
15.	b	57
16.	b	59
17.	c	63
18.	d	63
19.	d	63
20.	b	65
21.	a	66
22.	c	69
23.	a	70
24.	c	59
25.	d	72

CHAPTER 4

Judaism and Christianity

Overview: Both Christian theology, with its appeal to the downtrodden, and the Christian church, drawing on Roman administrative practices, were propelled to success largely by late imperial social, economic, and intellectual conditions. Whether in these years Christianity, as a religion, weakened or strengthened Rome prior to its eventual collapse, the church did, later, become the steward of Rome's legacies in both western and eastern Europe.

From its original appeal to Jewish messianism, Christianity, under the tutelage of St. Paul, was translated into a doctrine with some appeal to many peoples and was transported to Asia Minor, Greece, and Italy itself. Roman persecution of Christianity was, though intermittent, inevitable given the refusal of Christians to perform the few patriotic rituals demanded by the civic religion of the empire. What was far from inevitable was the ultimate triumph of Christianity during the fourth century, when it was first tolerated and later sanctioned as the official state religion of Rome. This success owes, in part, to the ability of Christianity to ingest and synthesize elements of many of its rival mystery religions.

Once embraced by Rome, the church spread throughout the empire, and its operations ceased being clandestine. The church's ambivalence toward Rome, even after the edicts of Constantine and Theodosius, can be seen in the monastic movement and the writings of Jerome, Augustine, and others. As western Rome declined, the papacy, in line of descent from Augustus no less than from St. Peter, began a consolidation of power which would culminate in the papal monarchy of the Middle Ages.

KEY TERMS FOR DISCUSSION

episkopos	Petrine theory
mystery religions	monasticism
Judeo-Christianity	Eucharist
evangel	Caesaropapism
toleration	syncretism

SELF-CHECK EXERCISES: After reading the chapter, you may wish to monitor your retention of the material with the following questions.

1. A mystery religion which originated in Persia and was especially popular with the Roman military was the cult of

    a. Cybele
    b. Isis
    c. Mithra
    d. Bacchus

2. A philosophy with substantial appeal to Roman intellectuals and to the upper classes and which asserted that "each human soul makes a pilgrimage toward an eventual union with the divine spiritual essence" was

    a. Stoicism
    b. Christianity
    c. Epicureanism
    d. Neoplatonism

3. Which is being described: They made war on the territories adjoining Judea, forcibly circumcising non-Jewish men, and added greatly to the anti-Jewish feelings already powerful among the gentiles of the Mediterranean seacoast and across the Jordan River. To complaints they replied that they were reestablishing themselves in the land of their ancestors.

    a. Seleucids
    b. Hasmoneans
    c. Antigonids
    d. Assidaeans

4. A party within Judaism which "lived in a monastic community, shared communal property, believed utlimately that wickedness would end and the poor in spirit prevail and, in general, had much in common with yet-to-appear Christianity" were the

      a. Essenes   c. Pharisees
      b. Saducees   d. Zealots

5. Christianity in the Pauline version stressed all but which of the following:

      a. baptism
      b. salvation by faith
      c. communion
      d. ecstatic denial of the world

6. A policy of relatively lenient treatment of the early church was instituted by the emperor

      a. Trajan   c. Hadrian
      b. Vespasian   d. Claudius

7. Of all the persecuting emperors, the most harsh and systematic was

      a. Nero   c. Diocletian
      b. Decius   d. Valerian

8. Who is being described: Though he continued to appease the sun god as well as the god of the Christians, he regarded himself as a Christian. Before his death in **337**, it became state policy to return all confiscated church lands.

      a. Maxentius   c. Julian
      b. Constantine   d. Theodosius

9. "Is there any thing whereof it may be said, see this is new? It hath been already of old time, which was before us." This passage comes from the

      a. Gospel of Mark
      b. Book of Jonah
      c. Epistles of Paul
      d. Book of Ecclesiastes

10. One of the earliest accounts of the Christian sect (termed "a most mischievous superstition"), written prior to any of the Gospels and describing Nero's persecutions is in the writings of

    a. Tacitus
    b. Seneca
    c. Pliny
    d. Lactantius

11. In the eastern part of the empire, church authority was from the start vested in the

    a. patriarch
    b. congregation
    c. papacy
    d. emperor

12. Which was not a feature of the earliest eastern monastic rules?

    a. celibacy
    b. work
    c. evangelism
    d. poverty

13. An early heresy asserting that association with corrupt Rome had tainted the church and rendered its sacraments invalid was

    a. Donatism
    b. Manichaeanism
    c. Gnosticism
    d. Arianism

14. Who is being described: Christianizing much that he found in the classics, he transformed Cicero's stoic concept of duty to the state into a Christian concept of duty to God. As bishop of Milan, he publicly humiliated the emperor Theodosius and forced him to do penance for savagely punishing some rioters.

    a. Jerome
    b. Basil
    c. Ambrose
    d. Cassiodorus

15. Christianity's responsibility for Rome's demise is refuted in

    a. Augustine's City of God
    b. the Nicene Creed
    c. the Rule of Benedict
    d. Augustine's Confessions

ANSWER KEY, WITH PAGE REFERENCES IN THE TEXT

	Answer	Page
1.	c	74
2.	d	75
3.	b	76
4.	a	77
5.	d	79
6.	a	80
7.	c	81
8.	b	82
9.	d	80
10.	a	81
11.	d	83
12.	c	84
13.	a	86
14.	c	88
15.	a	90

CHAPTER 5

The Early Middle Ages in Western Europe

Overview: Roman civilization declined and evolved, if it did not truly "fall." Barbarians, indeed, provided a kind of solution to late Roman decrepitude, and many early medieval practices and institutions clearly are blendings of Roman and (largely German) barbarian elements. A good example is the political consolidation of the Franks, through the time of Charlemagne, a process that literally began as western Rome was expiring but which allowed for the revival of the imperial idea and its conveyance into Medieval times.

In politics and economics, feudalism and manorialism were progressive Roman-German compounds which withstood the disruptive aspects of the Viking or Norman invasions. These, to be sure, had a constructive aspect--the Normans created efficient, lasting governments in parts of Europe as far-removed as Britain and Russia.

Likewise, the civilization of early Medieval Europe was a blend of Roman and barbarian elements productive of enough energy and accomplishment as to call into serious question the concept "Dark Ages." Church and state alike, especially in the time of Charlemagne, worked to preserve and convey the classical tradition, while at the same time vernacular languages were nonetheless replacing Latin in both popular speech and in literature.

KEY TERMS FOR DISCUSSION

    barbarians   missi dominici

    Medieval   feudalism

    autarky   manorialism

    Arianism   Dark Ages

SELF-CHECK EXERCISES: After reading all or part of the chapter, you may wish to check your retention with the following questions.

1. According to the text, the best term for the years 500 to 1000 is

       a. late Antiquity   c. the Dark Ages
       b. the Renaissance   d. the early Middle
                                                         Ages

2. The primary reason for the Goths' encroachment on Roman territory seems to have been to

       a. gain access to Roman technology
       b. escape the Hunnic incursions
       c. gain access to the Mediterranean
       d. adopt Roman institutions

3. During the general cultural collapse of the fifth century, learning and the arts flourished in

       a. Visigothic Spain   c. Vandalusia
       b. Celtic Ireland   d. Northumbria

4. The traditional date and event marking the end of the western Roman Empire was the

       a. Visigothic sack of Rome in 410
       b. Vandal sack of Rome in 455
       c. deposition of Romulus Augustulus in 476
       d. death of Theodoric in 526

5. Early Frankish rulers, beginning with Clovis, accomplished all but which of the following?

    a. displaced Roman and Gothic rivals
    b. won support of the Roman clergy
    c. checked the Muslim advance in Europe
    d. withstood the internal threat of the Pepins

6. Gregory I made the papacy a strong and active institution, but failed to
    a. suppress the Lombards
    b. establish monasteries
    c. administer the city of Rome
    d. send missionaries to Britain

7. Historians who praise the accomplishments of Charlemagne usually consider his greatest achievement to be his

    a. christianization of the Saxons
    b. coronation as Roman emperor
    c. establishment of the Spanish march
    d. personal style of administration

8. Many historians feel that Charlemagne's reestablishment of imperial power contributed significantly to

    a. secular dominance of the church
    b. separation of church and state
    c. religious dominance of the state
    d. suppression of individual rights

9. The political climate after Charlemagne's death could be described as all but which of the following?

    a. treacherous
    b. coalescing into large units
    c. splintering into small units
    d. unstable

10. Which is cited as the chief motive for the invasions of the Northmen?

    a. desire for booty   c. wanderlust
    b. polygamy   d. overpopulation

11. The Normans are known to have founded efficient administrative structures in all but which locale?

    a. North America   c. Russia
    b. Normandy   d. Italy

12. According to the text, feudalism could be described as all but which of the following?

    a. local   c. personal
    b. systematic   d. improvised

13. Early Medieval agriculture benefited greatly from

    a. the three-field system
    b. the horse shoe
    c. the wheeled plow
    d. all of the above

14. The Capitulare de Villis provided for all but which of the following?

    a. penalties for theft and murder
    b. tithes for all churches
    c. independent estates
    d. supplies for womens' work-shops

15. Legally, a serf was bound to

    a. the king   c. the land
    b. a lord   d. the church

16. Within a manor, land belonging to the lord was called the

    a. escheat   c. heriot
    b. villis   d. demesne

17. The post-Roman decline of arts and letters was brought on by

    a. deterioration of communication
    b. rise of vernacular languages
    c. collapse of town life
    d. all of the above

18. Boethius kept alive some remnants of the classical tradition by all but which of the following?

    a. studying and translating Aristotle
    b. holding the post of consul
    c. his philosophic writings
    d. his Arian writings

19. Copying, and therefore preserving, classical literary texts is credited to which early sixth-century figure?

    a. Justinian
    b. Cassiodorus
    c. Theodoric
    d. Gregory the Great

20. Charlemagne's court boasted a fine palace school, thanks primarily to

    a. Sidonius
    b. Bede
    c. Alcuin of York
    d. Gregory of Tours

===

USING THE CHAPTER'S DOCUMENTARY RESOURCES

<u>On page 107, see the boxed document</u>: The <u>Capitulare de Villis</u> is one of over seventy surviving edicts from during or just after the time of Charlemagne. They are sometimes called "circular letters," and were carried by Carolingian <u>missi</u> to the domains of counts and bishops, where they were to have general applicability as the regulations of the emperor. Some writers have contended that the capitularies are more a guide to the plans or goals of Carolingian administration than to the actual operations of manorial economies. In them, we find a picture of what autarky could have been like. Indeed, notions of the likelihood and extent of the autarky of the great estates are conjectures extrapolated from such documents. Scholars also feel the capitularies are probably modeled on Roman texts, further calling into question the degree to which they can be assumed to mirror ninth-century realities.

Thus, we must be content to view the <u>Capitulare de Villis</u> as an economic plan, but one which definitely illustrates the newly restored importance of the written word in Carolingian times, as well as (probably) the tendency to rely on classical textual models. We see here, at the very least, both the aspiration and the method for turning a chaotic Europe into an orderly one.

FOR DISCUSSION: How did the Capitulare de Villis, assuming it was in practice, foster manorial autarky? How did it also give evidence of imperial control from the center?

ANSWER KEY, WITH PAGE REFERENCES IN THE TEXT

	Answer	Page
1.	d	94
2.	b	95
3.	b	96
4.	c	98
5.	d	98
6.	a	98
7.	b	100
8.	b	102
9.	b	102
10.	d	102
11.	a	102
12.	b	105
13.	d	106
14.	c	107
15.	c	106
16.	d	106
17.	d	108
18.	d	108
19.	b	109
20.	c	110

CHAPTER 6

Byzantium and Islam

<u>Overview</u>: Some centuries after the collapse of Roman authority in the West, Medieval Europe could lay claim as a successor to Rome's imperial greatness, and in the time of Charlemagne (circa 800) such claims, if still audacious, had at least some substance. In the period between the collapse of western Rome and the rise of the Carolingian state, two other heirs of Rome, both in the East, exhibited far greater potential: the Byzantine, or East Roman state and the nascent civilization of Islam. Each made the early Medieval west appear backward by comparison. Constantinople was much older and prosperous and Baghdad more vital, ambitious, and expansionist than any of Rome's western successors.

Unfortunately for Byzantium and Islam, geographic proximity led to bitter competition and protracted conflict. Indirectly at least, the more backward West benefited from this strife by standing apart from it, at least until the onset of the Crusades around 1100, while also being able to incorporate many cultural and technological borrowings from the East.

In its status as a buffer between Europe and Asia, Byzantium occasionally suffered at the hands of each, and its decline may be said to owe to the compound effects of incursions by both the Mongols and the Crusaders in the 1200s. Before this, the Byzantine economy thrived on the monopoly of silk and other luxuries for which western Europe had developed a brisk demand. As Islam, from its base in Spain, stimulated the early medieval West, Byzantium provided the cultural matrix within which Kievan, and later Muscovite, Russia would develop.

KEY TERMS FOR DISCUSSION

    yokes

    Caesaropapism

    schism

    iconoclasm

    Rus

    hagiography

    Kaaba

    troubadours

SELF-CHECK EXERCISES: After reading the chapter, you may wish to monitor your retention of the material with the following questions.

1. Byzantine emperors traditionally bore all but which of the following titles:

   a. imperator
   b. basileus
   c. pontifex
   d. autocrat

2. In Justinian's codification of Roman law, an introduction to both the laws and their interpretation was provided in the

   a. Institutes
   b. Code
   c. Digests
   d. Novela

3. Byzantium withstood numerous sieges and incursions, including that of the ethnic group which eventually populated the Balkans, the

   a. Huns
   b. Pechenegs
   c. Slavs
   d. Varangians

4. Having thwarted many earlier assaults, Constantinople was sacked in 1204 by

   a. Normans
   b. Russians
   c. Mongols
   d. Crusaders

5. A state monopoly critical to Byzantine economic relations with the West was

   a. silk
   b. marble
   c. amber
   d. gold

6. The emperor who permanently enacted the Nicene Creed and was the last to rule over a truly unified East and West Rome was

    a. Alexius
    b. Theodosius
    c. Honorius
    d. Justinian

7. In 717-718, the Byzantine emperor Leo III is credited with

    a. defeating the Arab siege of Constantinople
    b. capturing Crete and Sicily
    c. forming an alliance with the Franks
    d. settling the monophysite controversy

8. In the struggle over iconoclasm, the greatest defenders of religious images were the

    a. emperors
    b. monks
    c. iconoclasts
    d. court eunuchs

9. The Byzantine "time of troubles," beginning in 1057, was characterized by all but which of the following:

    a. Byzantines ousted from Italy by Normans
    b. defeat by the Seljuk Turks in Armenia
    c. Magyar raids in the Balkans
    d. maintenance of Byzantine power in Armenia

10. In the text, it is asserted that the major Byzantine cultural achievement was

    a. transmission of their civilization to the Slavs
    b. theological innovations
    c. conversion of the Seljuk Turks to Christianity
    d. the theory of caesaropapism

11. The cyrillic alphabet derives from Byzantine missionary activity in

    a. Bulgaria
    b. Romania
    c. Russia
    d. Moravia

12. What nation is described in this chronicle passage? "There was no law among them ... discord thus ensued .... They accordingly went overseas to the Varangians and said 'Our whole land is great and rich, but there is no order in it. Come to rule and reign over us.'"

      a. Moravia   c. Russia
      b. Bulgaria   d. Serbia

13. Who is being described? He did not accept Orthodox Christianity until after he had sent a commission to various countries where other faiths were practiced. Shortly after receiving their report, he was baptized and married a Byzantine princess. Returning to Kiev, he threw down all the idols and forcibly baptized the entire population.

      a. Oleg   c. Vladimir
      b. Boris   d. Rurik

14. According to the text, one penalty paid by the Russians for conversion into the Greek Orthodox Church was

      a. cultural lag from using Slavonic rites
      b. spread of Greek at expense of Russian
      c. meager attention to spirituality
      d. severed ties with Scandinavia

15. One aspect of the Kievan Russian society which may have been more advanced than the Medieval West was its

      a. diplomacy   c. theology
      b. economy   d. military

16. According to the text, the aspect of God (Allah) most emphasized in Islam is his

      a. justice   c. mercy
      b. omnipotence   d. triune form

17. What is described? It is a concept very like the Christian crusade: those who die in battle against the infidel die in a holy cause.

    a. Hegira
    b. Haji
    c. Jihad
    d. Khalifa

18. Which is described? They opposed all reliance on Koranic commentaries; their faith was fundamentalist, and they were far more intolerant of the unbeliever than other Islamic sects.

    a. Yahtrib
    b. Shi'ites
    c. Sunnites
    d. Sufis

19. What ninth-century nation is being described? "My fellow Christians study the works of Moslem theologians and philosophers, not in order to refute them, but to acquire a correct and elegant Arabic style .... Who is there that studies the Gospels, the Prophets, the Apostles?"

    a. Persia
    b. Egypt
    c. Spain
    d. Arabia

20. Which is not a common feature of Islam, Judaism, and Christianity?

    a. monotheism
    b. individual prayer
    c. pilgrimage
    d. a holy book

ANSWER KEY, WITH PAGE REFERENCES IN THE TEXT

	Answer	Page
1.	c	116
2.	a	116
3.	c	117
4.	d	117
5.	a	119
6.	b	122
7.	a	123
8.	b	123
9.	d	123
10.	a	124
11.	d	124
12.	c	124
13.	c	125
14.	a	125
15.	b	126
16.	b	129
17.	c	131
18.	b	132
19.	c	133
20.	c	129

CHAPTER 7

Church and Society in the Medieval West

Overview: An agricultural revolution preceded and no doubt enabled virtually all Medieval progress, whether economic or cultural. With the growth of towns and the return of a monetary economy the stage was set for a renascence of culture in the twelfth century and, simultaneously, for the rise of such uniquely Medieval accomplishments as universities, the Gothic style and scholastic philosophy.

Politically, as well as culturally, the church dominated the nations of the West, giving rise to church-state conflict as strong kings and emperors appeared in Germany and, later, in France and England. A church which had to face the new realities of urbanizing societies, a changing and rapidly growing economy, and contentious secular authorities had, itself, to become a far more dynamic institution. Even the church's dominance in education faced challenges in the form of Abelard and Aquinas, as well as from interest groups and associations of academics and students. The world of the High Middle Ages had become far more complex, interesting, and challenging. Of all institutions, the church faced the greatest problems from this new reality.

The status of Medieval women rose in the twelfth century and after, with the spread of Mariolatry and courtly love, but the actual roles available to women within society were no different than those possibilities already open to Roman women--besides marriage and the family, only limited participation in business and religion.

The world of the High Middle Ages--complex, ambitious, and rapidly secularizing--was as different from the so-called Dark Ages as that time was from the cosmopolitan urbanism of ancient Athens or Rome.

KEY TERMS FOR DISCUSSION

bourgeois	auctoritas
bills of exchange	potestas
coronation	cardinals
Drang nach Osten	universals
scholasticism	Gothic style

SELF-CHECK EXERCISES: After reading the chapter, you may wish to monitor your retention of the material with the following questions.

1. According to the text, the eleventh century represented "a major turning point in the social and economic life of the West" for all but which of these reasons:

    a. Muslim and Norman raids were beginning
    b. life expectancies were increasing
    c. trade was beginning to revive
    d. the West took the offensive against Islam

2. In the text, the "first emancipation of women since the triumph of Christianity" is associated with all but which of the following:

    a. extension of education beyond handicrafts
    b. rise of Mariolatry
    c. celebration of courtly love
    d. popularity of nunneries

3. Which is not cited in the text as an element in the power of the Medieval church?

    a. its armies   c. excommunication
    b. its right to tax   d. interdict

4. St. Ambrose and the emperor Theodosius are participants in a very early example of

    a. coronation   c. confirmation
    b. excommunication   d. "render unto Caesar"

5. In the text, the term "simony" is defined as

    a. selling church offices
    b. theological heresy
    c. a lapse from chastity
    d. a turn toward secularism

6. In the Medieval West, a ruler who "controlled two or more kingdoms but did not claim supremacy over the whole world" was often termed

    a. rex
    b. emperor
    c. grand prince
    d. basileus

7. Who is being described? He used a seal with the words "Renewal of the Roman Empire." He tried to make imperial power real in Italy by putting German officials on church lands.

    a. Otto I
    b. Otto III
    c. Conrad I
    d. Conrad II

8. According to the text, the part of western Europe freest of feudal ties was

    a. Germany
    b. Italy
    c. France
    d. England

9. Who is being described? The Saxon nobles joined forces with the pope and made him promise to clear himself of excommunication on pain of the loss of his crown. To prevent a papal visit to Germany, he secretly went to Canossa, where the pope was staying. The pope kept him waiting three days, barefoot and in sackcloth, before allowing him to do penance and be absolved.

    a. Otto III
    b. Conrad II
    c. Theodosius
    d. Henry IV

10. The pope who called his own power like that of the sun and kingly power like that of the moon, and who came the closest to realizing papal monarchy was

    a. Gregory VII
    b. Alexander III
    c. Innocent III
    d. Honorius III

11. Which is described? They helped the sick and did useful, if humble actions in the world, rather than leaving it altogether. They wore neither splendid vestments nor hairshirts, but they preached, baptized, heard confessions, and helped the poor unobtrusively.

    a. Benedictines   c. Augustinians
    b. Cluniacs   d. Cistercians

12. In which order were all other duties subordinated to preaching?

    a. Franciscans   c. Cistercians
    b. Dominicans   d. Benedictines

13. Residence halls or "colleges" were first organized at the university of

    a. Bologna   c. Oxford
    b. Salerno   d. Paris

14. Who is being described? He argued that universals were not merely names, nor did they have a real existence. They were, he said, concepts and as such had a real existence of a special kind in the mind, which had created them out of its experience with particulars. His compromise between nominalism and realism is called conceptualism.

    a. Anselm   c. Abelard
    b. Aquinas   d. Averroes

15. A Medieval political writer who asserted, in his <u>Defensor Pacis</u>, that the "only true source of authority in a commonwealth was the <u>universitas</u> <u>civium</u>, the whole body of the citizens" was

    a. Aquinas   c. John of Salisbury
    b. Dante   d. Marsiglio of Padua

===

USING THE CHAPTER'S DOCUMENTARY RESOURCES

<u>On pages 138 and 140, see the boxed documents</u>: Though exceptions abound, the status of women in the Middle Ages continued to be an extremely beknighted one during an era which wedded the traditions of Greco-Roman and Germanic patriarchy to the full-blown misogyny of the church fathers.

Occasionally, scarcity of marriageable women accorded them bride gifts or courtly suitors but, in the main, women remained a powerless group with few extra-familial options that were socially acceptable. Long-run exploitation had led men to view women as inferior, and the inference drawn from inferiority was continued subordination.

Women as perpetually childlike, and consequently in need of discipline and instruction, is a recurring motif in Medieval (not to exclude earlier and subsequent) writings; as can be seen from the two documents at hand.

FOR DISCUSSION: From what is said, and unsaid, in these two documents, list a few tentative conclusions about the roles and status of Medieval women, and about men's attitudes toward women. From these documents, do you see any evidence for what is described in the text (page 187) as the "first emancipation of women since the triumph of Christianity"?

ANSWER KEY, WITH PAGE REFERENCES IN THE TEXT

	Answer	Page
1.	a	136
2.	d	138
3.	a	139
4.	b	140
5.	a	140
6.	b	141
7.	b	142
8.	a	142
9.	d	143
10.	c	145
11.	c	149
12.	b	149
13.	d	150
14.	c	151
15.	d	152

CHAPTER 8

The Beginnings of the Secular State

Overview: The earliest Medieval ingatherings of political power have been those of the Carolingian and Saxon emperors and the papacy. The claims of each were to imperial dominion over secular or spiritual affairs, or both.

The first experiments with what would come to be termed the nation-state also occurred in the Middle Ages. Both England and France exhibited dramatic growth in royal political power and in the administrative and bureaucratic buttresses necessary for the regular exercise of such power. From different starting points and by differing routes, but largely in response to one another's political affairs, England and France, from around the year 1000 until the conclusion of the Hundred Years' War in the 1450s, went from being intertwined feudal monarchies to being two of the earliest examples of ambitious, effective, and very nearly absolutist monarchy, though the Magna Carta kept England from a full-blown absolutism.

From tentative control over the Ile de France, the Capetians, in just over 300 years, extended royal authority over nearly all French territory, in the process ridding themselves almost entirely of the English presence on French soil. The end of the Capetian dynasty, however, presented the English with the opportunity to pursue their problematic claim to the throne of France. The intermittent hostilities of the Hundred Years' War produced great setbacks for the French, and after Henry V's victory at Agincourt the English claim was very nearly realized. By the time the combined efforts of Joan of Arc and Charles VII had again liberated France, both it and England were essentially free of papal authority and each had developed a lively vernacular literature.

KEY TERMS FOR DISCUSSION

Ile de France	Domesday Book
Albigensians	scutage
Inquisition	common law
provost	parliament
parlement	clockwork
ordonnance	chivalry
Estates-General	vernacular

SELF-CHECK EXERCISES: After reading the chapter, you may wish to monitor your retention of the material with the following questions.

1. According to the text, the first large and unified state in the medieval West was

    a. Spain
    b. France
    c. Italy
    d. Germany

2. Which is not cited as an advantage enjoyed by the early Capetian kings vis-a-vis their feudal vassals?

    a. they controlled more land
    b. they enjoyed the sanctity of kingship
    c. they were in partnership with the church
    d. their domain was compact and easy to govern

For items 3. through 6., give the name of the person who is described in the following quotations or paraphrases from the text. Choose from the following individuals:

Louis VI	Philip (II) Augustus
Louis IX	Charles VI
Hugh Capet	Philip IV

3. _____ When he came to the throne, there was little to distinguish him from the last feeble Carolingians. He was the first of a male line that was to continue uninterrupted for almost 350 years.

4. _____ He quadrupled the size of the French royal domain. He supported the revolt of the sons of Henry II of England. He later managed to ruin the reign of one of those sons, John, by wresting Normandy from the English after the battle of Buovines in 1214.

5. _____ Deeply pious, almost monastic in his personal life, he carried his high standards over into his role as king, and is viewed, as a perfect ruler. He dressed simply, gave aims, bathed lepers, built hospitals, and commissioned Sainte Chapelle. For such accomplishments, and for leading two crusades, he was sainted in 1297, less than thirty years after his death.

6. _____ His reign ushered in a trend toward centralization of administrative functions. He ruthlessly pushed the royal power into confrontation with towns, nobles, and the church. His humiliation of the papacy helped end the idea of a Christian commonwealth.

7. The greatest of all threats to the Capetians was that posed by

    a. the Angevin Empire
    b. the dukes of Normandy
    c. the <u>Curia Regis</u>
    d. the Holy Roman Empire

For items 8. through 10., give the name of the person who is described in the following quotations or paraphrases from the text. Choose from the following individuals:

Eleanor	Blanche
Julia	Matilda
Emma	Catherine

8. _____ An English queen, she married a great vassal of the French king, the count of Anjou. The reign of her son, Henry II, unified England, Normandy, Anjou and other territories into what is sometimes called the Angevin Empire.

9. _____ She had married Louis VII of France. After that marriage was annulled in 1152, she lost no time in marrying Henry II of England and adding Aquitaine to his already substantial French holdings.

10. _____ The daughter of a Norman duke, she married first the Anglo-Saxon king Ethelred and later the Danish king Canute. Wife of two English kings and mother of a future king by each of them, she apparently dominated all four, while remaining close to her Norman relatives. William the Conqueror was her great-nephew.

11. Which is described? A new sort of official, not resident in the countryside but tied to the court, who would travel about enforcing the king's will, rendering royal justice, and collecting taxes. He received no fief, and his office was not hereditary. He was a civil servant appointed by the king and paid a salary.

    a. viscount   c. enqueteur
    b. provost   d. bailiff

For items 12. and 13., give the name of the person who is described in the following quotations or paraphrases from the text. Choose from the following individuals:

    Innocent III   Clement V

    Boniface VIII   Martin V

12. _____ A Roman aristocrat and already an old man when elected pope, he suffered from a malady which kept him in great pain and probably accounted for his fierce language. For instance, he said he would rather be a dog than a Frenchman. He issued an edict instructing clerics to disobey kings and, in the bull <u>Unam sanctam</u>, pushed claims of papal authority even further, declaring that all people were the pope's subjects.

13. _____ A French pope, he never went to Rome. Instead he established the papal capital at Avignon, beginning the "Babylonian captivity" of the papacy. He reversed many earlier papal edicts and praised the French king for his piety.

14. Which statement about the <u>Magna Carta</u> is untrue?

    a. it was a feudal document
    b. it led to the notion that taxation must be by consent
    c. it made no concessions to townspeople or the church
    d. as soon as he had signed it, John tried to revoke the document

15. From which work of literature is this passage taken? "In a broad meadow below Aix-la-Chapelle the barons meet: their battle has begun. Both are courageous, both of them valiant lords... They charge and strike with all their might. Both shields are shattered, both chevaliers have fallen to the ground. The French lament, thinking their man must fall. 'O, God,' says Charles, 'now let the right prevail.'"

    a. <u>Canterbury Tales</u>
    b. <u>Song of Roland</u>
    c. <u>Beouwulf</u>
    d. <u>Chevalier de la Charette</u>

For items 16. through 20., give the name of the person who is described in the following quotations or paraphrases from the text. Choose from the following individuals:

Harold	Edward I	William
John	Richard	Henry II
Ethelred	Edward III	

16. _____ He had successfully asserted his rights in Normandy, allowing no castle to be built without his license. Because he put down private warfare and efficiently dispensed justice, there was peace and order. His invasion of England had the blessing of the papacy, which recognized his claim.

17. _____ Cutting at the roots of anarchy, he had more than 1100 unlicensed castles destroyed. He had appointed his friend, Becket, archbishop of Canterbury, but a great quarrel broke out between the two. After Becket's murder, he was forced to undergo a humiliating penance.

18. _____ He spent less than six months of his ten-year reign in England, but thanks to his father's bureaucracy there was efficient order even with the king on crusade. Indeed, heavy taxes were levied to support his crusading and his wars with France, not to mention his ransom from captivity.

19. _____ He exiled the Canterbury monks and confiscated their property. Innocent III responded by placing England under interdict and excommunicating him. He was forced to accede to papal demands, recognizing England and Ireland as papal fiefs and agreeing to pay annates to Rome.

20. _____ He enacted a great series of systematizing legal statutes, for which he is sometimes called "the English Justinian." His parliament of 1295 is traditionally called the Model Parliament because it included all classes of the kingdom, and had been summoned under the celebrated clause: "What touches all should be approved by all." Reflecting the decline of feudalism, he required all freemen to equip themselves for military service.

21. The French dynasty which replaced the last, largely inept Carolingians was the

        a. Valois
        b. Capetians
        c. Merovingians
        d. Normans

22. The French <u>parlements</u> functioned mainly as

        a. an arm of the inquisition
        b. provincial legislatures
        c. royal investigators
        d. judicial tribunals

23. A twelfth-century queen of first France and later England was

        a. Christine de Pisan
        b. Eleanor of Aquitaine
        c. Blanche of Castile
        d. Emma of Normandy

24. All English freemen were required to equip themselves for military service by

    a. Harold   c. Richard
    b. Henry II   d. Edward I

25. In the text, this work of literature is described as perhaps the first to bespeak "a patriotic note of love of country."

    a. <u>Beowulf</u>   c. <u>Song of Roland</u>
    b. <u>Canterbury Tales</u>   d. <u>Parsifal</u>

==

USING THE CHAPTER'S VISUAL RESOURCES

<u>On page 164, see the detail from the Bayeux Tapestry</u>: The Bayeux Tapestry, actually an embroidery, depicts the events leading to the Norman conquest of England--from Edward the Confessor's decision to invest William of Normandy as his successor through the climatic battle of Hastings, at which William's rival Harold was killed. The tapestry is housed in the Bayeux museum in Normandy and was probably commissioned by the bishop Odo of Bayeux, William's half brother, shortly after the events depicted. The tapestry was rediscovered in the eighteenth century and has been the subject of much attention ever since. For instance, Napoleon used the tapestry's depiction of William's exploits as a rallying point for his own planned invasion of England in 1803.

In the detail, William's knights are shown engaging Harold's own dismounted knights who, in order to strengthen their defensive position fought in this manner rather than on horseback. In their company can be seen one of the lightly armed archers who actually comprised the majority of Harold's force. On the shields of two of the Saxons can be seen crosses. William's men rode under the banner of the cross (unseen here), emblem of papal support for his cause. Thirty years later, Urban II would justify the First Crusade, in part, by decrying such internecine warfare among fellow Christians.

ANSWER KEY, WITH PAGE REFERENCES IN THE TEXT

	Answer	Page
1.	b	157
2.	a	158
3.	Hugh Capet	157
4.	Philip Augustus	158
5.	Louis IX	160
6.	Philip IV	161
7.	a	158
8.	Matilda	165
9.	Eleanor	158
10.	Emma	163
11.	d	160
12.	Boniface VIII	162
13.	Clement V	162
14.	c	166
15.	b	170
16.	William	163
17.	Henry II	165
18.	Richard	166
19.	John	166
20.	Edward I	169
21.	b	157
22.	d	160
23.	b	158
24.	d	169
25.	c	170

CHAPTER 9

The Late Middle Ages in Eastern Europe

Overview: The capture of Jerusalem in 1099 by the First Crusade represented a turning point in the development of the Medieval West, which had, by the end of the eleventh century become sufficiently well-ordered and secure as to engage in the only long-lived (though sporadic) European expansionism since the end of the Roman Empire. The Crusades likewise were testimony to the organizational powers of the papacy, at least in the case of the First Crusade. Subsequent crusades, often directed against fellow Christians in Asia Minor and Eastern Europe, were symptomatic, instead, of commercial or territorial greed. On balance, the Crusades both stimulated greatly the European demand for Eastern commodities and, paradoxically, devastated one of the prime sources for such imported luxuries, Constantinople.

In the East, the decline of the Byzantine Empire and the Caliphate of Baghdad produced only short-lived power vacuums. The Ottoman Empire, in a way, was successor to both Byzantium and Baghdad, while to the North, Muscovite Russia also was beginning to grow and to lay claim to the legacy of Eastern Rome.

The Ottoman consolidation over Byzantine territory and expansion into the heart of Central Europe presented the first grave threat to early modern, late Renaissance, Europe, and also represented the last of the great Asian incursions into Europe. Another of these incursions, that of the Mongols some 200 years earlier (circa 1240), had destroyed the Russian capital of Kiev and severed Russia's centuries-old commercial and cultural ties with an already declining Constantinople. Thus it was from Mongol and natively Russian roots that Muscovy developed.

KEY TERMS FOR DISCUSSION

plenary indulgence	capitulations
bazaar	serfdom
Outremer	Oprichnina
Hesychasm	zemski sobor
janissaries	cossacks

SELF-CHECK EXERCISES: After reading the chapter, you may wish to monitor your retention of the material with the following questions.

1. Which was not a cause or justification of the Crusades?

    a. the belief that pilgrimage would secure pardon from sin
    b. persecution of Christians and Jews in the Holy Land
    c. the legend of Charlemagne's protectorate
    d. the papacy's plans to reunify Christendom

2. Who is being described? He took Jerusalem by assault in July 1099, after which he allowed a slaughter of Muslims and Jews. He refused to accept a royal crown in the city where Christ had worn the crown of thorns, but he accepted the title "defender of the Holy Sepulcher."

    a. Peter the Hermit
    b. Godfrey de Bouillon
    c. Stephen of Blois
    d. Alexius Comnenus

3. Which is being described? A military order of knighthood, its members took vows of poverty, chastity and obedience, and wore red crosses on white tunics. Ultimately, they so completely forgot their original vows of poverty that they engaged in banking and large-scale finance. Their order was destroyed, in the early fourteenth century, by Philip IV of France for political reasons.

    a. Hospitalers   c. Teutonic Knights
    b. Templars   d. Cistercians

For items 4. through 7., give the name of the person who is described in the following quotations or paraphrases from the text. Choose from the following individuals:

        Saladin   Muhammed II

        Zangi   Suleiman I

        Tamerlane   Selim I

4. _____ The greatest Muslim leader of the Crusade period, he was a vigorous and successful general who was often moved by chivalrous and humane impulse. In 1187 he took Jerusalem, but signed a treaty with Richard of England allowing Christians to visit the city freely.

5. _____ With his accession to the Ottoman throne in 1451, the doom of Constantinople was sealed. After taking the city in 1453, he gave thanks to Allah in Hagia Sophia and ground the altar of the sanctuary beneath his feet; thenceforth, it was a mosque.

6. _____ He nearly doubled the size of the Ottoman Empire in Asia at the expense of the Persians and in Africa at the expense of Egypt, which was annexed in 1517.

7. _____ He resumed the Ottoman advance into Europe, participating in wars between the Hapsburgs and the Valois kings of France and affecting the Protestant Reformation by the threat of invasion from the southeast. He annexed Iraq and Algeria, took Belgrade and Buda, and besieged Vienna. In the Persian Gulf and Indian Ocean he fought naval wars with the Portugese.

8. Which is described? Innocent III called for a crusade, and the Venetians agreed to furnish transportation. The Venetians redirected the crusaders' efforts against Constantinople, which was twice sacked. The Venetians salvaged much, shipping back to their city, among other things, the great bronze horses now adorning St. Mark's. Horrified, the pope excommunicated the crusaders.

        a. First Crusade   c. Fourth Crusade
        b. Third Crusade   d. Sixth Crusade

9. Which is not a legacy of the Crusades?

    a. commercial concepts, and products
    b. prosperity of the Italian traders
    c. rise of banks
    d. inhibition of maritime exploration

10. Who is the speaker? "Remission of sins will be granted to those going thither .... Let those who are accustomed to wage private wars wastefully even against believers, go forth against the Infidels in a battle worthy to be now undertaken .... Let those who formerly contended against brothers and relations rightly fight barbarians."

    a. Urban II   c. Innocent III
    b. Gregory VII   d. Louis IX

11. After Kiev succumbed to the Mongols, the next long-lived center of Russian unity was

    a. Lithuania   c. Moscow
    b. Novgorod   d. Sarai

12. The most lasting effect of Tatar overlordship in Russia was

    a. in the arts   c. their law codes
    b. their engineering   d. their tribute system

13. Which was not a factor in the rise of Moscow?

    a. antagonism to the Orthodox church
    b. advantageous geographic location
    c. a line of remarkably able princes
    d. useful relations with Tatar overlords

For items 14. through 18., give the name of the person who is described in the following quotations or paraphrases from the text. Choose from the following individuals:

Vladimir   Michael Romanov   Nikon

Dmitrii Donskoi   Ivan IV   Avvakum

Ivan III   Boris Godunov

14. _____ He put himself forward as the heir of the princes of Kiev and declared that he intended to regain Russian lands lost to the Poles and Tatars. He married the niece of the last Byzantine emperor, adopted the Byzantine title "autocrat," and hired Italian architects to build the Kremlin.

15. _____ He succeeded to the throne as a small child. Later, he embarked on a period of strong government and institutional reform, convoking the first zemski sobor (land assembly). He extended Russian authority as far as Kazan and Astrakhan, opening the entire Volga to Russian commerce.

16. _____ Though a man of talent, he could not overcome handicaps: Ivan's legacy of disorder, the intrigues of the nobles, and a famine and plague that began in 1601. When a pretender arose under the protection of the Polish king, Russia was launched into the decade-long "Time of Troubles."

17. _____ A zemski sobor elected him czar, establishing a dynasty which would reign in Russia from 1613 to 1917. For the first ten years of his reign the zemski sobor remained in session, but it soon ceased to be summoned.

18. _____ He revised the Russian church ritual to bring it into line with Greek practice, which provoked a schism. He also argued that the authority of the patriarch, in spiritual affairs, exceeded that of the czar.

19. According to the text, the first foreigners to actually teach industrial techniques to the Russians were the

    a. English   c. Dutch
    b. Italians   d. Germans

20. The greatest support for Russia's westernization seems to have come from

    a. the church   c. the people
    b. the court   d. the nobility

ANSWER KEY, WITH PAGE REFERENCES IN THE TEXT

	Answer	Page
1.	c	175
2.	b	176
3.	b	177
4.	Saladin	177
5.	Muhammed II	183
6.	Selim I	184
7.	Suleiman I	184
8.	c	178
9.	d	180
10.	a	175
11.	c	187
12.	d	187
13.	a	188
14.	Ivan III	188
15.	Ivan IV	189
16.	Boris Godunov	189
17.	Michael Romanov	189
18.	Nikon	189
19.	a	190
20.	b	190

CHAPTER 10

The Rise of the Nation

Overview: A cluster of fourteenth-century calamities serves as the punctuation mark separating the Middle Ages and the Renaissance. Among these are the Hundred Years' War, the Great Schism in the church, and the most devastating pandemic in history, the Black Death. The Hundred Years' War accelerated already discernable tendencies in England and France toward consolidated national monarchies, while also eroding dramatically the position and the very ranks of feudal chivalry. Tendencies that would produce a fragmented Western Christendom were widespread during the several fourteenth-century crises gripping the church and, in the short run at least, the church's problems simply accelerated the ascent of already rampant monarchies. The Black Death destroyed the workings of the highly sophisticated late Medieval money economy and, in its aftermath, hastened the demise of serfdom, thus helping to insure a vastly different foundation for the fifteenth-century economic recovery.

The Hundred Years' War forms but one phase in the long-run growth of both the English and French monarchies. In Spain, progress toward monarchical absolutism came much more swiftly in the late fifteenth century, when the dynastic marriage of Ferdinand and Isabella (1469) and the completion of the seven-century-long reconquest (1492) ushered in a period of national greatness coupled with an extreme of enforced social conformity rarely exceeded in history.

In Italy, the political and economic environment that produced the Renaissance was woven from the interrelations of the great commercial cities Florence, Venice, and Milan. The contours of modern economics and diplomacy, rather than those of absolutism, were being drawn by the Italians.

KEY TERMS FOR DISCUSSION

Salic law	standing army	Hansa
Jacquerie	reconquest	condotierre
apanages	Cortes	Gallicanism
taille	elective monarchy	Great Schism

SELF-CHECK EXERCISES: After reading the chapter, you may wish to monitor your retention of the material with the following questions.

1. Which is <u>not</u> mentioned as an aspect of a "world turned upside down" at the transition from Medieval to modern?

    a. bastard feudalism
    b. new monarchy
    c. social stability
    d. monetized economy

2. The effects of the Black Death included all but which of the following?

    a. death of one third or more Europeans
    b. severe shortage of laborers
    c. artistic preoccupation with death
    d. decline of the medical arts

3. Despite other causes, the Hundred Years' War began directly as a result of

    a. Edward III's dynastic claims
    b. pressure from England's Flemish allies
    c. Philip IV's consolidation of power
    d. Valois' plans to invade England

4. Which is described? Despite inferior numbers, the English profited from French incompetence and their own reliance on large numbers of longbowmen who, from their high ground position, poured arrows on the French knights and mercenaries.

    a. Sluys   c. Crecy
    b. Bouvines   d. Montaperti

For items 5. through 7., give the name of the person who is described in the following quotations or paraphrases from the text. Choose from the following individuals:

    Edward I   Henry VII   Richard III

    Edward III   Henry VIII   Henry V

5. _____ His mother was a daughter of Philip IV, and he claimed that as nephew of the last Capetians he had a clearer right to succeed them than their cousin, Philip of Valois. He allied himself with the Flemish obligarchy and put forth his claim as king of France in 1337.

6. _____ Able, courageous, and ruthless, he continues to be the focus of much controversy, having been indelibly depicted as a villain by Shakespeare. He was slain in 1485 on Bosworth Field and the War of the Roses came to an end.

7. _____ His efficiency, avoidance of costly wars, and assistance to English merchants won support in the business community. He reestablished prosperity as well as law and order in an England weary of rebellion and civil war. He made the monarchy the rallying point of English nationalism and fixed the misleadingly labeled policy of "Tudor absolutism" toward Parliament.

8. The impetus for French success in the final stages of the Hundred Years' War came initially from

    a. Henry V   c. Joan of Arc
    b. Charles VII   d. Etienne Marcel

9. When the Hundred Years' War ended in 1453, the one remaining English possession in France was

    a. Bordeaux   c. Normandy
    b. Calais   d. the Aquitaine

For items 10. and 11., give the name of the person who is described. Choose from the following:

    Charles V   Louis XI

    Charles VI   Charles VII

10. _____ Because he was intermittently insane, his relations engaged in rivalry for power during his reign. After Agincourt, he declared his own son illegitimate and adopted Henry V of England as his heir.

11. _____ He energetically pursued the strong monarchical tradition of Philip Augustus and Philip IV, for instance, by raising taxes. He enlarged the army and shattered the hopes for a Burgundian kingdom. He recovered most of the apanages and laid the foundations for future French nationhood.

12. Who is described? Advocating a church without property, he called for direct access by the individual to God without priestly intermediaries. Despite the church's insistence that the Scriptures be read only in Latin, he translated the Bible into English. His views were condemned as heretical.

    a. Wycliffe
    b. Wolsey
    c. Becket
    d. More

13. "I found there friars, all the four orders, preaching to the people for profit of their bellies, interpreting the gospel as they well please.... Unless Holy Church now be better held together, the most mischief on earth will mount up fast." Who is the author of this allegorical dream?

    a. Wycliffe
    b. Chaucer
    c. Froissart
    d. Langland

14. All but which event occurred in the year 1492, referred to in the text as "the most crucial year in Spanish history."

    a. entry of Spanish monarchs into Granada
    b. abolition of the Cortes
    c. Columbus' first voyage of discovery
    d. persecution of unconverted Jews

15. The Great Schism was ended and the formal unity of western Christendom restored by

    a. Council of Pisa
    b. John Hus
    c. Council of Constance
    d. Gregory XI

16. Who is described? A Spanish pope, he made notable progress in subjugating the lords of central Italy and breaking the power of the Roman princely families. He was greatly aided by his son Cesare, the alleged hero of Machiavelli's The Prince.

    a. Martin V   c. Sixtus IV
    b. Alexander VI   d. Julius II

17. According to the text, the political lessons of Renaissance Italy--the "school of Europe"--were first distilled by Niccolo Machiavelli in

    a. The Discourses
    b. The Prince
    c. The History of Florence
    d. Mandragola

For items 18. through 20., select the city being described from the following:

    Venice   Florence

    Siena   Milan

    Rome   Ravenna

18. _____ It lay in the midst of the fertile plain of Lombardy and was the terminus of trade routes through the Alpine passes. It was also a metal-working center, famous for its weapons and armor. The precarious balance of its republican politics was upset by the Visconti power seizure.

19. _____ A pioneering center of industry and finance, its urban commune had acquired the dominant political position in the twelfth century. After Edward III repudiated his debts to its banks, social unrest persisted and reached a climax with the revolution of the Ciompi in 1378. By the 1430s power had passed to a champion of the poor: Cosimo de' Medici.

20. _____ Its political stability contrasted with other cities' turbulence. Called the Republic of St. Mark, it was in fact an empire controlling the upper Adriatic and parts of Greece. Having no landed nobility, its government reflected the city's commercial interests.

ANSWER KEY, WITH PAGE REFERENCES IN THE TEXT

	Answer	Page
1.	c	195
2.	d	196
3.	b	198
4.	c	199
5.	Edward III	198
6.	Richard III	205
7.	Henry VII	206
8.	c	200
9.	b	201
10.	Charles VI	199
11.	Louis XI	201
12.	a	204
13.	d	204
14.	b	206
15.	c	210
16.	b	211
17.	b	214
18.	Milan	211
19.	Florence	212
20.	Venice	213

CHAPTER 11

The Renaissance

Overview: It was the nineteenth century which formalized the now common view of the history of western civilization as divided into the eras, or periods, of ancient, medieval, and modern. While people living at the height of the Roman Empire did not consider themselves "ancient," and an individual living in the Middle Ages could have had no awareness of what he or she was living "between," people living at the dawn of the modern age did have some appreciation of this fact and, in Italy, applied the term Rinascita (rebirth) to it around 1550. Even earlier, Petrarch had, around 1350, coined the term "Dark Age" to set off his own striving and energetic times from all which stood between himself and the end of antiquity, for whose revival--or rebirth--he, Petrarch, strove so devotedly.

What was reborn was an interest in and appreciation of the relevancy of the Roman, and later also the Greek, classics in the prosperous Italian cities of the early fourteenth century. In Italy there was a closer relationship to the classical past than elsewhere in western Europe. Italians lived literally amid the ruins of the Roman Empire. The revival came at this point in time because the Florentines, Milanese, Sienese, and others saw their own civilization as the first great urban age in a thousand years and, therefore, were much interested in whatever could be learned from an examination of their "roots" in Roman civilization. An element of nationalism was present in the Italians' attempt to assert the primacy of their history and institutions over the more recent association with the German emperors.

The Renaissance itself, hard hit by the onset of the Black Death in 1347-1348, had to be reborn around 1450, after which time it gave color and texture to a hundred years of political, economic, and religious life.

KEY TERMS FOR DISCUSSION

    Ciompi   italics

    florins   polyphony

    enclosure   chiaroscuro

    humanism   Palladian style

<u>SELF-CHECK EXERCISES</u>: After reading the chapter, you may wish to monitor your retention of the material with the following questions.

1. The shift of primary European trade routes from the Baltic to the Atlantic tended to favor the commerce of

    a. Venice   c. the Hansa
    b. Novgorod   d. England

2. The most lastingly important event in the mid-fifteenth century seems to have been

    a. the fall of Constantinople
    b. the marriage of Ferdinand and Isabella
    c. the invention of printing
    d. the renascence of the papacy

3. The ancient writer who developed the concept <u>studia humanitatis</u>, or humanism, later so dear to the Renaissance, was

    a. Vergil   c. Boethius
    b. Cicero   d. Plato

4. Which was <u>not</u> true of Renaissance painting:

    a. it remained subordinate to architecture
    b. patrons of the arts and the pagan gods and heroes of antiquity became subjects for paintings
    c. use of perspective became widespread
    d. oil paint became a typical medium

For items 5. through 13., give the name of the person who is either described in or who is the author of the following quotations from the text. Some names may be used more than once. Choose from the following individuals:

Rabelais	Ficino
Erasmus	da Vinci
Dante	Cellini
Valla	Petrarch
Boccaccio	Pico della Mirandola

5. _____ The first major Italian writer to embody some of the qualities that were to characterize Renaissance literature .... but much of his outlook bore the stamp of the Middle Ages, including the chivalric concept of disembodied love inspiring his devotion to Beatrice. His hostility to the political ambitions of Boniface VIII expresses the reaction of a Christian who wanted the pope to keep out of politics.

6. _____ Lived for a time at the worldly papal court in Avignon .... as a professional man of letters he collected and copied the manuscripts of ancient authors, produced the first accurate edition of the Roman historian Livy, and found ... forgotten letters by Cicero .... He so admired the past that he addressed a series of affectionate letters to Cicero and other Roman worthies .... He wrote countless sonnets in the Italian vernacular to his adored Laura, whom he courted in vain until she died during the Black Death.

7. _____ He turned to letters after his apprenticeship in banking left him disillusioned with business practices .... His distress at the clergy's neglect of manuscripts and their corruption made him strongly anticlerical, a theme in his <u>Decameron</u>, the first major prose work in the Italian vernacular, which recounts stories told by a group of young Florentines who have moved to a country villa during the Black Death.

8. _____ He commanded both immense learning and the courage to use it against the most sacred targets. He criticized the supposedly flawless prose of Cicero ... and his own expert knowledge of Latin led him to point out errors in the Vulgate Bible .... his fame rests above all on his demonstration that the Donation of Constantine, one basis for justifying papal claims to temporal domination, was a forgery.

9. _____ A medical student turned classicist, he was entrusted by Cosimo de' Medici to translate Plato. Humanity, he wrote, has the unique faculty called intellect, which he described as an "eye turned toward the intelligible light," or God. He coined the term <u>Platonic</u> <u>love</u> to describe the love that transcends the senses ....

10. _____ Ficino's pupil, he knew Arabic, Hebrew, Greek, and Latin. His tolerance was as broad as his learning ... and he helped to found the humane studies of comparative religion and comparative philosophy .... in his final years, he gave away his world possessions and became a supporter of Savonarola.

11. _____ Called the "Prince of the Humanists," he coupled a detached view of human nature with faith in the dignity of humanity .... a tireless advocate of his "philosophy of Christ," he nevertheless helped to destroy the universality of Catholicism. Perhaps because he sought compromise, he has also become enormously popular with twentieth-century humanists.

12. _____ He contributed far more to literature than the salacious wit for which he became famous. He studied the classics, practiced and taught medicine, and created two of the great comic figures of letters--Gargantua and his son Pantagruel. His credo, "Do what thou wilt," was not an invitation to sloth. To him free will meant self-improvement on a grand scale.

13. _____ He exemplifies both the short-comings and the achievements of Renaissance science. Taking hit-or-miss notes in a secretive left-handed writing, he had little concern for publication of his findings and speculations .... He had a passionate curiosity about almost everything concerning human beings and nature.

For items 14. through 16., give the name of the person who is described. Choose from the following:

  Michelangelo   Holbein

  Durer   Botticelli

  Titian

14. _____ When commissioned by the Medici to do <u>The Birth of Venus</u> (1485), he made the goddess, emerging full grown from a

seashell, more ethereal than sensual, and he placed the figures in the arrangement usual for the baptism of Christ.

15. _____ Best known as a sculptor, he ranks among the immortals of painting as a result of one prodigious achievement--the frescoes he executed for the Sistine Chapel in the Vatican.

16. _____ Identified with Lutheranism in his later years, he created what has been termed the first great Protestant art, in which he simplified traditional Christian themes by pruning them of what Lutherans regarded as Catholic trimmings .... fascination with nature led him to include wild creatures in many pictures ... and his improvements in the techniques of woodcuts and engravings enabled him to mass-produce his own drawings as illustrations for printed books. He was the first best-selling artist.

17. According to the text, a round-the-clock operation with three eight-hour shifts was pioneered in the

    a. Hapsburg silver mines
    b. Venice arsenal
    c. Florence textile workshops
    d. cities of the Hansa

18. When the English king Edward III defaulted on his debts in the 1340s, the impact was felt primarily by the bankers of

    a. London   c. Siena
    b. Amsterdam   d. Florence

19. According to the text, Erasmus is most accurately described as a

    a. conserver of classical culture
    b. vernacular writer
    c. neo-pagan writer
    d. synthesizer of Christian and classic writings

20. Theophrastus Bombastus von Hohenheim, who first proposed that chemical remedies be applied to specific diseases, is better known as

    a. Galen   c. Vesalius
    b. Paracelsus   d. Agricola

==
USING THE CHAPTER'S VISUAL RESOURCES

<u>On page 213, see the portrait bust of Lorenzo de' Medici and on page 230, the painting "Primavera" by Botticelli</u>: Of all patrons of Renaissance art outside the church, Lorenzo is probably the most famous--in launching the careers of da Vinci, Michelangelo, and Filippo Lippi, as well as Botticelli. He was himself an accomplished writer of poetry and prose and a diletante architect, but is best-known as the sponsor of Verocchio's studio and school for young artists as well as the patron of numerous works of sculpture, painting and architecture.

Verocchio's portrait bust was done when Lorenzo was approximately thirty-five and had already been manager of the Medici banks for fifteen years. In the sitter's stern but purposeful visage we can see something of the gravity of Lorenzo's position. Two years earlier, he had been an intended victim in an assassination plot in which his less fortunate brother, Giuliano, had been killed. The vendetta which followed was just ending, so a trace of vengeance may also be detected.

No one's paintings hold a more important place in the story of the classical revival in art than those of Sandro Botticelli. The "Primavera," commissioned by the Medici family, shows an interest in classical mythology and in stylized but unblushing nudity. It was this "creeping paganism" in all the arts that became one of the targets of Savonarola just a few years later, and Botticelli came under his spell, consigning numerous of his paintings to the bonfires of the vanities. Botticelli's works were called by Walter Pater, a nineteenth century champion of Renaissance aesthetics, a "direct inlet to the Greek temper."

ANSWER KEY, WITH PAGE REFERENCES IN THE TEXT

	Answer	Page
1.	d	218
2.	c	220
3.	b	221
4.	a	227
5.	Dante	221
6.	Petrarch	221
7.	Boccaccio	221
8.	Valla	222
9.	Ficino	222
10.	Pico della Mirandola	222
11.	Erasmus	223
12.	Rabelais	223
13.	da Vinci	224
14.	Botticelli	228
15.	Michelangelo	229
16.	Durer	229
17.	a	219
18.	d	219
19.	d	223
20.	b	225

CHAPTER 12

The Protestant Reformation

Overview: Parallel to the rise of absolute or nearly absolute monarchies was the decline of the one institution most antithetical to the growth of royal power, the church. In the sixteenth century, in a variety of nations and for differing, though often similar reasons, the unity of Western Christendom was broken.

Under diverse banners of "protest" and "reform," movements sharing a wish to vastly diminish if not destroy the power of Rome and the wish to both reorder and relax church ritual and organization gained strength, though all had to sooner or later put behind their rebellious origins.

Of all Protestant leaders, the most fractious was Luther, whose movement was as much a national as a religious one. In this sense, Luther was the true successor to both Wycliffe and Hus, as he himself, when pushed to do so, acknowledged. The other large-scale national separation from Rome was accomplished by the English king, Henry VIII. Unlike Luther, whom he despised, Henry sought to remain utterly Catholic, but to become head of his own church, a ploy which, together with his confiscation of monastic property, vastly increased both his power and wealth.

John Calvin's movement was based more on class than on national interests, and was the first international alternative to Catholicism in Europe. If Luther's appeal was to Germans, Calvin's was to the nascent bourgeoisie, and Calvinist sects began to appear throughout Europe. Besides its place in the history of religion, Calvinism, identified in several theories with the rise of capitalism, also holds a prominent place in some accounts of European economic history.

KEY TERMS FOR DISCUSSION

indulgences	bonfires of vanities
identity crisis	priesthood of all believers
Erastianism	Pilgrim's Progress
Index	Protestant Ethic
Anabaptists	cuius regio, eius religo
Ein feste Burg	Act of Supremacy

SELF-CHECK EXERCISES: After reading the chapter, you may wish to monitor your retention of the material with the following questions.

1. According to the text, the most accurate term for the early Protestant leaders is

    a. reformers
    b. rebels
    c. revolutionaries
    d. reactionaries

2. Who was the author of the <u>Imitation of Christ</u>, a mystical work "addressed to the inner life of the individual"?

    a. Thomas a Kempis
    b. John Wycliffe
    c. Desiderius Erasmus
    d. Johan Huizinga

3. Which statement about Girolamo Savonarola is untrue?

    a. his eloquent sermons made him the most affecting and influential preacher in Florence
    b. his popularity forced the papacy to recognize his power in Florence
    c. he organized troops of children to root out the "vanities" in Florence
    d. he referred to Alexander VI as a "monster" presiding over a "harlot church"

4. Among the reasons contributing to Luther's success may be counted all but which of the following?

    a. his ideas had broad appeal in Germany
    b. his success profited the princes financially
    c. the emperor Charles V was forced to compromise in the matter of German religion
    d. the papacy constantly ignored him

5. What is described? This sixteenth-century German uprising was led by educated men who had a program, a set of revolutionary ideas of what the new social structure should be. Their leaders drew up a series of demands.

    a. formation of the League of Schmalkalden
    b. abolition of the Teutonic Order
    c. uprising of knights
    d. peasants' rebellion

6. In establishing the Church of England, Henry VIII accomplished all but which of the following:

    a. retention of Catholic doctrine and ritual
    b. abolition of monasteries
    c. fundamental alterations in doctrine
    d. denied the supremacy of the pope

7. Which is described? They pushed the doctrine of justification by faith to its logical extreme in anarchism: each person was to find God's universal law within the private conscience. They did not believe in class distinctions or private property.

    a. Antinomianism   c. Socinianism
    b. Unitarianism   d. Erastianism

8. Which is described? They are identified with the rejection of the trinity as an irrational concept, and with the view that Christ was simply an inspired human being.

    a. Calvinists   c. Baptists
    b. Lutherans   d. Unitarians

9. Among the common denominators of Protestantism were all but which of the following?

    a. a tolerant attitude toward fellow reformers
    b. repudiation of Rome's claim to be the one true faith
    c. less emphasis on religious externals like ritual and organization
    d. rebel origins

10. The Roman Catholic responses to the Reformation included all but which of the following?

    a. suppression of all rebels
    b. new priestly orders like the Jesuits
    c. compromise with leaders of new sects
    d. reaffirmation of doctrine of indulgences

Associate the following statements or quotations with either **Martin Luther (L)** or **John Calvin (C)**.

11. ___ His parents were of peasant stock. His authoritarian father became a prosperous investor and, ambitious for his son, sent him to the university of Erfurt to study law.

12. ___ He succeeded because the printing press made his ideas accessible and because those ideas, such as his attack on exploitation by Italians, appealed to all Germans.

13. ___ He shaped the Protestant movement as a faith and a way of life, and gave it a broadly European basis.

14. ___ His Institutes of the Christian Religion laid the doctrinal foundations for a Protestantism that broke completely with Roman organization and ritual. The very title Institutes reflects his legal training, and suggests Justinian's code.

15. ___ A specific abuse he sought to prove un-Christian was the "sale" of indulgences, in particular the activities of the Dominican Tetzel.

16. ___ He set about organizing his city of God, making Geneva a Protestant Rome, a magnet for Protestant refugees from many parts of Europe.

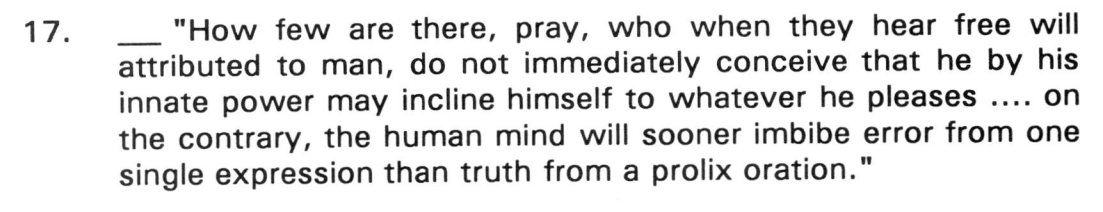

17. ___ "How few are there, pray, who when they hear free will attributed to man, do not immediately conceive that he by his innate power may incline himself to whatever he pleases .... on the contrary, the human mind will sooner imbibe error from one single expression than truth from a prolix oration."

18. ___ He underwent a prolonged and intense personal crisis of the type the psychoanalyst Erik Erikson has termed an identity crisis.

19. ___ "For Rome is the greatest thief and robber that has ever appeared on earth, or ever will .... We were born to be masters ... and should cease to be the puppet of the Roman pontiff."

20. ___ He did not found his separate church as an alternative to Rome, but as the one true church, and usually took over existing church buildings ... and soon the princes were superintending the process of converting the willing and evicting the unwilling.

ANSWER KEY, WITH PAGE REFERENCES IN THE TEXT

	Answer	Page
1.	c	237
2.	a	238
3.	b	238
4.	d	240
5.	d	242
6.	c	244
7.	a	245
8.	d	245
9.	a	245
10.	c	248
11.	L	238
12.	L	241
13.	C	243
14.	C	243
15.	L	238
16.	C	243
17.	C	246
18.	L	238
19.	L	240
20.	L	241

CHAPTER 13

The Great Powers in Conflict

Overview: In the sixteenth century, modern statecraft first appeared with its amalgam of diplomacy, land and naval warfare, global concerns, and generally expansionist policies that is still the foundation of international affairs in the twentieth century. Together with the aesthetic and attitudinal changes seen in the Renaissance and Reformation, and the stridently capitalist and mercantilist economic basis of European society, the new political realities of absolutism and bureaucracy, and the exercise of power, internally and externally, by aggressively sovereign states usher in the "modern world."

The first truly "great" power of the new era was Spain, and the principal architect of Spanish power from the 1550s until the end of the century was the hard-working, bureaucratically-oriented Philip II. During his long reign, covering half of Spain's "golden" century, all of the Iberian peninsula, the Netherlands, almost the entire Western Hemisphere, and parts of Asia and Africa were under Spanish control, forming the first "world" empire worthy of the name. Accompanying, and no doubt fostering, this greatness was the creation of one of Europe's first models of bureaucratic absolutism.

By century's end, Spain was entering a lengthy decline from its status as a great power, a process stretching to the 1890s. In the seventeenth century, France, England, and the Netherlands (now free of Spanish control) all eclipsed Spain. Each, though a latecomer to the game of empire, developed policies more conducive to gaining and managing specie and currency, the stock of which had grown over five hundred percent as a result of Spain's plunder of New World gold and silver. The mercantilist economies and the empiricists of the Scientific Revolution were forging modern institutions and temperaments as the fires of religious strife were finally banked after the Thirty Years' War.

KEY TERMS FOR DISCUSSION

sovereignty	mercantilism
Black Legend	price revolution
international law	Edict of Nantes
bureaucracy	induction
absolutism	rationalism

SELF-CHECK EXERCISES: After reading the chapter, you may wish to monitor your retention of the material with the following questions.

1. Which is <u>not</u> cited as a possible date and event separating Medieval and modern times?

    a. the discovery of America in 1492
    b. Luther's 1517 attack on the Roman church
    c. Copernicus' heliocentric theory of 1543
    d. the fall of Constantinople in 1453

2. According to the text, the apparatus of interstate politics was developed in Renaissance Italy, primarily in

    a. Venice
    b. Rome
    c. Milan
    d. Florence

3. According to the text, the "decisive step toward Dutch independence from Spain" was

    a. Alva's expedition
    b. the Antwerp massacre
    c. the defeat of the Armada
    d. the assassination of William the Silent

4. Though mercantilism was perfected in seventeenth century France, it was pioneered by sixteenth century

    a. Spain
    b. Holland
    c. England
    d. Italy

5. "We permit those of the so-called Reformed religion to live and dwell in all the towns and districts of this our kingdom without being annoyed or restrained. We ordain that there shall be no distinction, because of religion in the reception of students to be instructed in universities, or of the sick and poor into hospitals and charitable institutions...." This passage comes from an edict of

    a. Henry VIII
    b. Elizabeth
    c. Henry IV
    d. Philip II

6. The Dutch position as "economic pacesetter of seventeenth century Europe" was maintained by all but which of the following:

    a. the largest merchant fleet in the world
    b. scientific farming
    c. the East India Company
    d. control of New World silver mines

7. Which statement about the Peace of Westphalia (1648) is untrue?

    a. the right of dissidents to emigrate was recognized
    b. the Holy Roman Empire was strengthened
    c. what is sometimes termed the "first world war" came to an end
    d. the independence of the Dutch republic was recognized

8. The largest field army since Roman days, active during the Thirty Years' War, belonged to

    a. Sweden
    b. France
    c. the Empire
    d. Spain

9. Who is described? He became embroiled with the church by ridiculing ancient authorities. By 1610 he was using a telescope to study the heavens. Working from his experiments, others developed such instruments as the thermometer and the barometer.

    a. Leeuwenhoek
    b. Galileo
    c. Pascal
    d. Rabelais

10. Who is described? In 1687, he published the laws of motion as part of his Principia Mathematica. Many of his findings he had made two decades earlier while an undergraduate at Cambridge. He promoted the development of optics, but his greatest contribution to science was the law of gravitation.

    a. Boyle   c. Newton
    b. Kepler   d. Leibniz

11. Who is the author? "The power of judging aright and of distinguishing truth from error, which is called reason, is by nature equal in all men .... The diversity of our opinions, consequently, does not arise from some being endowed with a larger share of reason than others, but solely from conducting our thoughts along different ways."

    a. Newton   c. Bacon
    b. Descartes   d. Spinoza

For items 12. through 20., give the name of the person described. Choose from the following:

Mary Tudor	Catherine de' Medici
Henry IV	Elizabeth I
Henry VIII	Francis I
Philip II	Charles VIII
Charles V	Philip IV

12. _____ He inherited from his father, Louis XI, a well-filled treasury and a good army. Secure on the home front, he decided to invade Italy because it was rich and divided politically. It was easily conquered, but his acquisitions threatened the balance of power, and a coalition formed against him.

13. _____ He inherited Spain, the Low Countries, and the Hapsburg lands. He had France squeezed in a vice, which he sought to close. In 1527, his army besieged and sacked Rome.

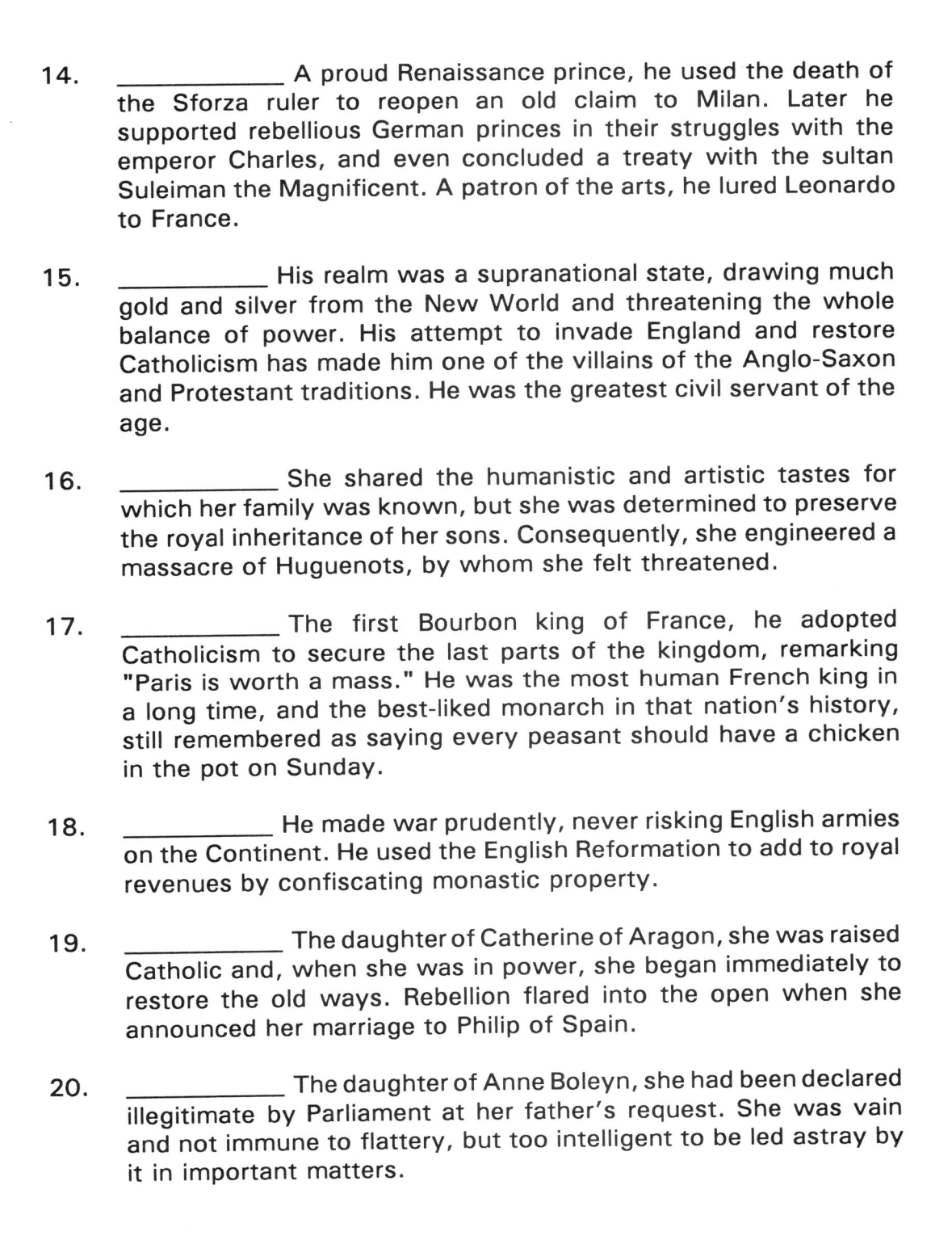

14. _____ A proud Renaissance prince, he used the death of the Sforza ruler to reopen an old claim to Milan. Later he supported rebellious German princes in their struggles with the emperor Charles, and even concluded a treaty with the sultan Suleiman the Magnificent. A patron of the arts, he lured Leonardo to France.

15. _____ His realm was a supranational state, drawing much gold and silver from the New World and threatening the whole balance of power. His attempt to invade England and restore Catholicism has made him one of the villains of the Anglo-Saxon and Protestant traditions. He was the greatest civil servant of the age.

16. _____ She shared the humanistic and artistic tastes for which her family was known, but she was determined to preserve the royal inheritance of her sons. Consequently, she engineered a massacre of Huguenots, by whom she felt threatened.

17. _____ The first Bourbon king of France, he adopted Catholicism to secure the last parts of the kingdom, remarking "Paris is worth a mass." He was the most human French king in a long time, and the best-liked monarch in that nation's history, still remembered as saying every peasant should have a chicken in the pot on Sunday.

18. _____ He made war prudently, never risking English armies on the Continent. He used the English Reformation to add to royal revenues by confiscating monastic property.

19. _____ The daughter of Catherine of Aragon, she was raised Catholic and, when she was in power, she began immediately to restore the old ways. Rebellion flared into the open when she announced her marriage to Philip of Spain.

20. _____ The daughter of Anne Boleyn, she had been declared illegitimate by Parliament at her father's request. She was vain and not immune to flattery, but too intelligent to be led astray by it in important matters.

ANSWER KEY, WITH PAGE REFERENCES IN THE TEXT

	Answer	Page
1.	d	256
2.	a	259
3.	c	262
4.	a	263
5.	c	267
6.	d	272
7.	b	276
8.	a	275
9.	b	278
10.	c	279
11.	b	279
12.	Charles VIII	260
13.	Charles V	260
14.	Francis I	260
15.	Philip II	261
16.	Catherine de' Medici	266
17.	Henry IV	267
18.	Henry VIII	268
19.	Mary Tudor	268
20.	Elizabeth I	269

CHAPTER 14

Exploration and Expansion

Overview: A phenomenon, sometimes called the Age of Discovery, spanning the years 1450 to 1600, resulted in the triumph of commercial capitalism in Europe and the expansion of European power into most other parts of the world. Thus were produced colonial holdings which, in some cases, have only been dismantled in the last thirty years. Interestingly, the first colonial power, Portugal, survived to be also the last such power to retreat from India and Africa.

In the process of discovery and empire-building, the most famous name is, of course, Christopher Columbus. In the wake of his four voyages, not only Spain but most European nations took an interest in and began to acquire overseas possessions, took in vast new wealth, and began to behave like merchants--hence the term "mercantilism." Like many of his well-known contemporaries, Columbus (1451-1506) was a "Renaissance man." Like the Medici, he was very acquisitive; like the humanists, he placed great store in the classics (at least the classical geographers); like the creative artists of his day, he consciously sought fame.

The Spanish and Portugese claims to, respectively, the New World and Africa produced the first international agreement of the new age of imperialism, the Treaty of Tordesillas (1494), negotiated by the papacy. Excluded from this division of spoils were all other European powers; however, the subsequent explorations under the flags of England, France, and the Netherlands all resulted in gains for these new participants. A final element in the general European expansion was Russia's exploration and settlement of Siberia, making it the first European nation to establish permanent relations with China, the original lure for the wave of exploration.

KEY TERMS FOR DISCUSSION

the known world	Tordesillas
compass	conquistadores
nirvana	disease frontier
mandarins	Nerchinsk
encomienda	Europeanize

SELF-CHECK EXERCISES: After reading the chapter, you may wish to monitor your retention of the material with the following questions.

1. According to the text, modern Western expansion differed in four ways from earlier similar examples. Which of the following was <u>not</u> one of them?

    a. it was much faster and covered more ground
    b. it led to a truly worldwide arena for European imperialism
    c. all the important sea voyages progressed along continental coastlines via pilotage
    d. it carried Westerners well beyond their familiar cultural orbit

2. Which was <u>not</u> mentioned among the motives for the acquisition of empire?

    a. curiosity about geography
    b. desire for glory
    c. hunger for gold
    d. strategic needs of nations

3. In Asia, the greatest European missionary success apparently occurred in areas which were primarily

    a. Muslim c. Confucian
    b. Hindu   d. Buddhist

4. Who is the writer? "I found very many islands peopled with inhabitants beyond number, which I first took for the mainland of Cathay .... In the earth there are many mines of metals ... there could be no believing, without seeing, such harbours as are

here.... The people all go naked, just as their mothers bring them forth."

    a. Columbus   c. Vespucci
    b. Dias   d. Cabral

5. Whose voyage is described? "We entered the Pacific, where we remained three months without taking on provisions .... We drank water yellow and impure and ate oxhides. Of rats, some of us could not get enough. I believe that nevermore will any man undertake to make such a voyage."

    a. Drake   c. Cabot
    b. Magellan   d. Verrazano

6. Who is described? He unsuccessfully attempted to found a settlement on Roanoke Island (in present-day North Carolina) in an area the English named Virginia, after their Virgin Queen, Elizabeth.

    a. Raleigh   c. Gilbert
    b. Drake   d. Hawkins

7. Which is credited with having salvaged the Jamestown colony?

    a. furs   c. tobacco
    b. corn   d. cotton

8. By the eighteenth century, European "taste" had been revolutionized by all of the following except

    a. tea   c. potatoes
    b. coffee   d. chocolate

For items 9. through 12., give the name of the person described. Choose from the following:

Magellan	Vespucci
da Gama	Prince Henry
Verrazano	Columbus
Cabot	Albuquerque

9. _____ An organizing genius who directed the work of others, he may well have been moved above all else by the desire to convert the populations of India and the Far East. He also hoped to break the Arabs' monopoly over the trade in gold from sub-Saharan Africa.

10. _____ Self-educated in geography, he was an experienced sailor. He had sailed parts of the African coast and as far north as Iceland. His central obsession, that the Far East could be reached by sailing westward, was not unique.

11. _____ He was most effective in spreading thin print about the New World and himself made a voyage to the mouth of the Amazon. His letters came to the attention of Waldseemuller, on whose maps the term "America" first appeared.

12. _____ A Portuguese in Spanish service, he set out in 1519 with a royal commission to find a way westward to the Spice Islands. He crossed the Pacific in a voyage of incredible hardship, and was killed in the Philippines.

For items 13. through 15., give the name of the area described. Choose from the following:

Asia	North America	South America
Africa	India	

13. _____ The Portuguese were contemptuous of the indigenous people once discovering they were not Christians. Its rulers had little hold over the regions of the South, where Europeans first established their footholds. All the European powers found it easy to win princes to their side and to raise and train native armies.

14. _____ It was never annexed by a European power and never lost its sovereignty. Its ancient civilization had repeatedly been subject to barbarian incursions, and was in the habit of absorbing them.

15. _____ The toll in lives for exploration here was staggering, and the sea passages were often horrendous, but unlike some other areas, its cultures crumbled under the impact of the Europeans.

ANSWER KEY, WITH PAGE REFERENCES IN THE TEXT

	Answer	Page
1.	c	283
2.	a	283
3.	d	290
4.	a	291
5.	b	293
6.	a	295
7.	c	295
8.	c	300
9.	Prince Henry	283
10.	Columbus	290
11.	Vespucci	291
12.	Magellan	292
13.	India	287
14.	China	288
15.	South America	292

CHAPTER 15

The Problem of Divine–Right Monarchy

Overview: European monarchies in the Middle Ages typically drew support from, and were consequently somewhat limited by, the church and the feudal nobility. Collectively, these three institutions--royalty, nobility, and clergy--made up the state, which in turn governed the powerless town dwellers and the agricultural peasants, who were often enserfed. The weakening of both the church and the nobility in the fourteenth through sixteenth centuries, as well as the wealth accumulated by some monarchs during the commercial revolution, paved the way for absolute monarchy in nations where both social unity and royal ambition were present.

Divine right monarchy was an embellishment of absolutism made possible by the position kings had assumed as head of both state and church, even in nations, such as France, which remained primarily Catholic. The remark attributed to Louis XIV, "I am the state," could be termed the virtual motto of Bourbon dynastic absolutism; moreover, the question concerning whether the king actually made this statement is unimportant, since he in any event acted in its spirit throughout his maturity as king.

One of the fullest theoretical defenses of absolutism is in the writings of Thomas Hobbes, who wished for such strong and orderly government in the turbulent England of the mid-seventeenth century. But it was John Locke's notion of limited government which gained ascendancy in England following the vicissitudes of the Stuarts and the Protectorate.

KEY TERMS FOR DISCUSSION

divine right	cultural imperialism
raison d'etat	Martinet
intendants	Asiento
Fronde	Puritanism
Versailles	Star Chamber
L'etat c'est moi	Rump Parliament
Gobelins	interregnum
Canal du Midi	Navigation Acts
blue laws	Bill of Rights
natural order	salon
Baroque	classicism
witchcraft	nobility of the robe

SELF-CHECK EXERCISES: After reading the chapter, you may wish to monitor your retention of the material with the following questions.

1. After 1648, the main force jeopardizing the European balance of power was

    a. Habsburg Austria
    b. Restoration England
    c. German Protestants
    d. Bourbon France

2. The most unstable nation, politically, in seventeenth century Europe was probably

    a. Russia b. Spain
    c. Sweden d. England

3. Which was <u>not</u> among the goals of Richelieu?

   a. to keep nobility subordinate to the king
   b. to compromise with the Huguenots
   c. to foster a sense of French greatness
   d. to make the monarchy more than just theoretically absolute

4. Under the Bourbons, the prime symbol of common French identity was

   a. the monarchy   b. language
   c. religion   d. culture

5. This 1709 battle in the War of Spanish Succession was typical of Louis XIV's military defeats in the latter years of his reign; each side sustained over 20,000 casualties in carnage not exceeded until the Napoleonic Wars. It was the battle of

   a. Boyne   b. Malplaquet
   c. La Hogue   d. Blenheim

For items 6. through 10., give the name of the person described. Choose from the following:

| Fouquet | Louis XIV | Louis XIII | Marie Louise |
| Colbert | Richelieu | Marie de' Medici | Mazarin |

6. _____ She served as regent but showed little political skill. Her Italian favorites and French nobles, Catholic and Huguenot alike, carried on a hectic competition that threatened to undo all Henry IV had accomplished.

7. _____ An efficient administrator as bishop of Autun but tired of provincial life, he moved to Paris and worked assiduously to gain a high position during the regency. He emerged as conciliator between the king and his mother and ultimately rose to the positions of cardinal and chief minister, virtually ruling France for nearly twenty years.

8. _____ Handpicked to be Richelieu's successor, he managed French affairs during the minority of Louis XIV, amassing an immense personal fortune.

9. _____ He had been badly frightened during the Fronde when rioters broke into his bedroom, and was determined to suppress all challenges to his authority. By education, temperament, and physique he was ideally suited to the role of grand monarque.

10. _____ The great French practitioner of mercantilism, he advanced rapidly to become controller general. He was influential in all matters of the French economy, but was always the king's collaborator, never his master.

11. Which group is described? Sometimes called the Puritans of the Catholic Church, they were a high-minded group who took an almost Calvinist stand on predestination. They questioned the authority of both king and pope, and attacked the pope's agents, the Jesuits.

    a. Huguenots
    b. Jansenists
    c. Quietists
    d. Frondists

12. Which group is described? They found many sympathizers in the revolutionary army and advanced a program later carried by emigrants to the American colonies: political democracy, universal suffrage, regularly summoned parliaments, progressive taxation, separation of church and state, and the protection of the individual against arbitrary arrest.

    a. Levelers
    b. Ranters
    c. Diggers
    d. Millenarians

13. The major steps necessary after 1689 to convert Britain into a parliamentary democracy with an only symbolic monarchy included all but which of the following:

    a. abolition of mercantilism
    b. a cabinet headed by a prime minister
    c. establishment of universal suffrage
    d. abolition of the House of Lords' veto power

14. Who is described? He was a close associate of the leaders of the Glorious Revolution whose relative optimism and enthusiasm for constitutional government were expressed in his Second Treatise of Government. He was an intellectual forebear of both the American and French revolutions.

a. Hobbes	b. Bodin
c. Locke	d. Bossuet

15. Who is described? The century's most controversial thinker, he was the son of a Jewish merchant in Amsterdam. He tried to reconcile the god of science with the god of scripture. He asserted that god was present everywhere in everything, but his pantheism led to ostracism and he found few admirers until the nineteenth century.

a. Pascal	b. Leibniz
c. Descartes	d. Spinoza

For items 16. through 20., give the name of the person described. Choose from the following:

| Charles I | Marlborough | William | James II |
| Charles II | Cromwell | James I | Coke |

16. _____ He was a well-educated pedant, sure of himself and, above all, certain that he ruled by divine right. He totally lacked the Tudor heartiness and tact, and was an object of distrust to his English subjects.

17. _____ He financed his war with France by a forced loan and by quartering troops in private houses at the owners' expense. Consequently, Parliament passed the Petition of Right, the "Stuart Magna Carta" which, among other things, expressly forbid taxation without consent of Parliament.

18. _____ He could not master the Rump Parliament, and forced its dissolution by appearing with a body of soldiers. As Lord Protector, he provided England with the only written constitution in its history.

19. _____ His reign was a period of moral looseness, lively court life, and Restoration drama with its ribald wit. But he dissipated much public good will by following a foreign policy which appeared subservient to Louis XIV.

20. _____ He accepted the invitation to take the English crown, which he was to share with his wife. When he landed on the Devon coast, James fled, giving him an almost bloodless victory.

ANSWER KEY, WITH PAGE REFERENCES IN THE TEXT

	Answer	Page
1.	d	306
2.	d	306
3.	b	307
4.	a	308
5.	b	315
6.	Marie de' Medici	307
7.	Richelieu	307
8.	Mazarin	309
9.	Louis XIV	309
10.	Colbert	313
11.	b	312
12.	a	322
13.	a	325
14.	c	326
15.	d	327
16.	James I	316
17.	Charles I	317
18.	Cromwel	321
19.	Charles II	324
20.	William	324